VOICES

VOICES

Canadian Writers of African Descent

AYANNA BLACK, EDITOR

HarperPerennial
HarperCollins*PublishersLtd*

The cover motif is inspired by a wood-carved Bangwa (Cameroon) house-post from the collection of Museum für Völkerkunde, Munich.

First Edition

Canadian Cataloguing in Publication Data

Main entry under title: Voices: Canadian writers of African descent

HarperPerennial ed.
ISBN 0-00-647413-6

1. Short stories, Canadian (English) - Black - Canadian authors.* 2. Short stories, Canadian (English) - 20th century.* 3. Canadian fiction (English) - 20th century.* I. Black, Ayanna.
PS8235.B55V64 1992   C813'.010896 C92-094105-2
PR9197.33.B55V64 1992

92 93 94 95 96 ❖ RRD 5 4 3 2 1

Acknowledgements

To each author, thank you for your trust and the opportunity to edit this collection. I wish to thank Austin Clarke, who encouraged me to do this book after I had organized a 1991 series of readings for Canadian Artists' Network—Black Artists in Action (CAN:BAIA). Thanks to Paul Savoie for translating Dany Laferrière's work, and Pat Jeffries for nourishing the computer with texts till the wee hours of the morning. Also, thank you to Barbara Berson, Maya Mavjee, Rebecca Vogan, everyone at HarperCollins, and everyone at CAN:BAIA. To Roberta Morris and Judith Fitzgerald, thank you for your suggestions, support and humour when I needed it most, just before the alarm sounded: Deadline.

Pull off the mask...and let myself emerge...born into new life, strengthened...and refreshed...

—Lorris Elliott

Thank you, Lorris, for your great contribution to black literature in Canada.

Contents

Foreword

We come from Jamaica, Trinidad, Barbados, Ghana, Haiti, Guyana, Nigeria, Canada, the United States and South Africa. As writers, we push the limits of literature and redefine images of representation. In the process, we create our realities. We are a new generation of *griots*—town criers, or spiritual messengers—whose stories have been transferred to the printed page. Despite the diversity of our cultural backgrounds, we write out of a collective African consciousness—a consciousness embodied in the fabric of oral traditions, woven from one generation to the next, through myths, storytelling, fables, proverbs, rituals, worksongs and sermons meshed with Western literary forms.

African-Canadian literary form has existed for at least two centuries, and began with the importation of slaves in Quebec and the arrival of escaped American slaves in Nova Scotia and southern Ontario. According to George Elliott Clarke's *Fire on the Water: An Anthology of Black Nova Scotian Writings*, the texts of Nova Scotian John Marrant, a former slave, date back to 1785, and are the earliest known writings of a black living in Canada. The more recent influx of immigrants from the Caribbean to

Canada in the nineteen-fifties, sixties and seventies, and lately the arrival of Africans, has created a highly textured literary quilt. This complex history—of a shared heritage on the continent, and the experiences borne of our dispersal to various parts of the world—were very much in my mind when the idea for *Voices* took root.

Voices presents new works of poetry and fiction by fifteen Canadian writers of African descent. In compiling this collection, I chose not to force the work into a preconceived moral, political or social framework. Rather, I was interested in providing a less structured, more open frame, to allow for the juxtaposition of individual and unique voices, ideas, styles and forms. I hope that I have acted as a catalyst for the articulation of an individual ethos.

The oral tradition is central to African writing, and so we begin with Molara Ogundipe-Leslie's "Garlands to the Beheaded One," a poem historically linked to the African call-and-response tradition. The poet vocalizes two or more lines alone, and is answered by a chorus. Norma De Haarte's folk tale likewise finds its roots in a more traditional, story-telling form. The latter voices of this collection, notably Claire Harris and Frederick Ward, draw the African aesthetic through an experimental fabric, creating a new texture.

Black writers are now, it seems, struggling between the political and personal landscapes in their work, and this struggle is a strong and recurring theme throughout *Voices*. Two stories, Makeda Silvera's "Her Head a Village" and Dany Laferrierè's "Why Must a Negro Writer Always Be Political?" are strong literal depictions of this contemporary struggle. Historically, African-Canadian writing has been overtly political, with little reference to the romantic or erotic. In *Canada in Us Now*, Harold Head writes: "There are no poems on roses or teacups.

The love poems have a certain edge to them. Rejecting the teachings of their colonial youth where poetry was placed in some higher metaphysical sphere, Black creative expression is designed to inspire and serve people."

Today, however, such exclusively exterior writing, in which we respond only to the issues that ignore the interior space, the core, is no longer. In *Yearning*, bell hooks points out that "psychological pain is...a central revolutionary frontier for black folks." She correctly identifies the need to heal ourselves, " 'cause you can't effectively resist domination when you are messed up."

Voices attempts to balance and to synthesize the exterior and interior spaces: the languages of romantic and sexual love, the languages of lesbianism, sexual abuse and abandonment. In this context, the personal is political, especially when examined from the perspective of a history of oppression. At this stage in the development of an African-Canadian literary aesthetic, the exposure of the deeply personal should be viewed as revolutionary— yes, revolutionary. We all speak passionately, venomously; and we write with immense pride, commitment and confidence. We are, as writers, first and foremost liberators of minds and bodies, not necessarily or primarily political liberators. We have learned true liberation can only be achieved through the freeing of the spirit.

Voices Voiced Voicing
Sounds Images Imagine Compose
mouths speech singing shouting
Drums Incantations Drums

AYANNA BLACK
Editor

Molara Ogundipe-Leslie

Garlands to the Beheaded One
praisesong to the true thalaiva
(thoughts after Rajiv Gandhi's assassination)

My thoughts keep coming back to you,
unknown and unsung woman,
sister of wonder, the beheaded one
garlanded with death,
you exploded death like forest pods
to self and others,
exploding yourself in mystery,
shouting: *"thalaiva! thalaiva!"*
My thoughts stop dead at your severed head!

Poet: *Ye-e-pa!*
Audience: *E ma wo o-o-o*

Severed in violence, from love or will or both
what courage lay stubborn within you, held you brave,
as they packed you electrified into a mule of death
what totalness! what zeal!

to so self-scatter to the four winds of the earth
what driving rage! what cause ! what steely need!

Poet: *Iku de!*
Audience: *E ma wo—o-o*

Woman garlanded with death, for death
my garlands of awe petrify here
in faraway Toronto
blow fragrances of awe to you softly
irrelevantly
my song enfolding not the dreams of India
inscribed in Rajiv for him by him or
through him but shrouding you
my song searches only you
forgotten one, unknown soldier
scattered to a charboiled death

Poet: *Ye-e-e pa!*
Audience: *E ma wo o-o-o-o*

Sliced to a staring icon,
your head sitting in formaldehyde
my distant thoughts throw petals
of awe at you and your dare,
woman of will, take petals from
women of your kind, take garlands!
praise the true thalaiva! name her here!
garland the true thalaiva! make way!

Poet: *E ma a wo o-o-o*
Audience: *E ma a wo o-o-o*

....

Ye—e-e-pa! is a Yoruba exclamation of grief.

Iku de! means "Death is here."

E ma wo is a prolonged way to say "Don't look at her." It is a ritual cry used in traditional sacred processions to clear the way. When the intonation on *ma* is varied, the meaning of the sentence becomes "Keep your gaze on her."

Thalaiva is an indian word for "leader."

Because We Are Mad
(song to a black sister in Chicago)

Because we dare to love
in a world without love
        in fear of love
        afraid to love
I laugh in weeping down the street
because I know
I met you somewhere before

I always felt that
someone like you lived
not only in the flesh-veils
of my heart but
lurking in the trees
the woods the grasses' hair
laughing somewhere freely
in the winds
free child of Nature
woman

non-threatening soft and true
I know because I know
I met you somewhere before

I laugh quietly through my pores
as I see you now absent
weeping through the skin of my eyes
I know I made my peace with you
a long time ago

a long, long time ago
five thousand years ago
in a green and happy land
where the spirits of light
kiss and dance
with the spirits of grace
and lotuses sit on becalmed water
balanced

They may say
that we are mad
I often think that we are mad
and I know
that we are mad
who seek to romp on
in a green and happy land
set by us in the asphalt sea
set about by jungles of monetary rage
steel and razor hands of global
violences
hands affixed
to the amputated souls

of our barons at home
our barons of home—made death

We are mad
who seek to find a light-filled place
resisting well
who seek to dance in its green and gold
to hug in the joy with which we know
the spirits of grace do melt
into the spirits of life

Norma De Haarte

Little Abu, The Boy Who Knew Too Much

Long, long ago in the lush, tropical country of Guyana, land of many waters, there was a boy named Abu. Abu lived on an island in the Esseequibo River in the county of Esseequibo. Hundreds of islands are clustered along the river, especially at the mouth. But many of these islands are uninhabitable. However, Abu lived on one of the largest, called Leguan, situated where the swift-flowing river current meets the Atlantic Ocean.

Abu's parents had been brought to the island as slaves from Africa, but like many others, they remained on the island when they were freed. After Emancipation, most of the people on the island purchased large plots of land from plantation owners and stayed on the island, working as farmers in their own right. Their main crops of sugar cane, rice and coconuts, from which oil was made, were chiefly for export, while vegetables and ground provisions were grown for domestic use. Cattle farmers sold cattle, milk, meat and hides to the region around, as far as the city of Georgetown.

Abu's parents had purchased large plots of land. However, bit by bit, his father leased or sold most of the land and kept only the lot on which the house was built. He also kept a few head of cattle.

Old Abu was not interested in farming. He had learnt the secret nature and effects of certain plants, berries and roots. This knowledge, which he brought from Africa, deepened with the abundance and rich variety of tropical shrubs, vines, berries and flowering plants.

When people had headache, fever, couldn't eat or sleep, and felt depressed, if they were bitten by venomous snakes or insects, scratched by poisonous plants, he administered "bush medicines"—potions, brews and teas. In this manner, he allevi-ated pain and stress, eliminated poisons from the body and restored his clients to health. Consequently, people travelled for miles from the farthest corner of the island and the far reaches of the coastlands to pay Old Abu a visit and tell him their problems.

In those days, there were no doctors to look after the slaves or indentured servants. Old Abu, therefore, provided an impor-tant service, necessary for the survival of the community. Without this service, many people would have died for lack of care, and the population of the island would have been deci-mated. Therefore, as natural as day is to night, tropical flora is to fauna, Old Abu was essential to the well-being of the people in the region around.

Even as a young boy, Little Abu began to learn these secrets from his father. He was not interested in farming as were the boys in the village. But when the village boys went with parents and relatives down to the "backdam" to work on their farms, Little Abu went and worked alongside them. If anyone was slashed by razor grass or a sharp tool, bitten by poisonous snakes or insects, or injured by cantankerous cattle, Little Abu was as resourceful as his father. He treated the wound with crushed leaves, berries and moss, then bound it securely with special leaves and vines. The boys in the village were in awe of Little Abu. They had the greatest respect for him.

During the planting and harvesting season, children did not attend school. Every child went down to the backdam. Those who were capable worked side by side with parents, until seedlings were sown or the harvest reaped. It was not unusual for neighbours to pitch in and help each other until the work was done. Even though Little Abu's parents did not farm on a large scale, Little Abu accompanied his friends and their parents down to the "back."

Early in the morning, when it was still pitch-dark, the boys would stop near Little Abu's house on their way, to call him with a pre-arranged signal. Hoot...Hoot...Hoot...Hoot...Hoot... Hoot...Hooot...Hoot or Kiss...Kiss...Kiss...Ka...dee! Three times they would utter the throaty cry of the owl or the clear trilling song of the kiskadee. Then they would move on slowly down the country road to wait. In nothing more than a few minutes, Little Abu would join them, shouldering a rice bag like the other boys.

Every boy enjoyed being in the backdam because it wasn't all hard work. The outdoors provided lots of interest and fun. Just before the sun was right overhead, everyone stopped for a meal and a rest. This was the cue the boys were awaiting. The ocean surrounding the island, the inlets and streams, even the waters of the rice or sugar-cane fields were teeming with fish. With bare hands, small baskets or nets, the boys would "catch and toss" fish to each other, returning to the waters the ones that weren't good enough or the right type. This was exciting sport!

On the other hand, some boys preferred the taste of fowl—
goose, turkey or pheasant—which roamed wild and in great
flocks, abundant on the island. With great care, the boys would
set about making snares to entrap their prey. But it was more
thrilling to separate a few birds from the wily flock. The plan
was to surround the birds infantry style, run them down in one
direction, then back again until the birds were tired. Then the
boys closed in on the exhausted prey.

While returning from these pursuits, a few boys would
spread out to gather fruit. They might collect fruit from their
own trees or carry out a raid on their neighbour's, depending on
which looked better. In those days no one minded as long as
trees weren't damaged or destroyed. They chose from the best
mangoes, guavas, pineapples, oranges, tangerines, papaws,
dunks, genips, psidium, golden, star, custard and monkey apples,
the last along with the luscious purple jamoons that grew wild
on the island. They picked whatever took their fancy.

But the real contest began when they decided to pick water
coconuts. After suitable trees were selected, they raced to see
who would be the first to shinny up the trees, with bare hands.
Sometimes each boy mounted the long, straight, barrel-like
trunk carrying a short, sharp pointed prod or cutlass between the
teeth. Many boys performed this difficult task with great ease
and flourish. But it was not unusual for a boy to lose his grasp,
fall and become seriously injured.

When fruit was collected from the ground or picked off
trees, the boys were very cautious. Care was taken to use long,
pliant sticks to prod the ground around the fruit in order to drive
away small poisonous snakes, hidden between leaves and fruit.
Leaves and branches of trees provide a camouflage for vipers and
stinging insects. No boy ventured anywhere without a stick for
protection. These boys worked hard on the land, but found ways

to make life interesting, while the land yielded its bounty.

Many stories were exchanged, repeated and handed down from one generation to the other, as a result of these experiences and escapades. Sometimes a few did not have happy endings.

Little Abu worked hard alongside his friends, but he was more interested in the animals, insects and plants around him. Sometimes he would lie stretched out on the grassy dam or under a coconut tree, noticeably absorbed as he lay still, listening, hand cupped to his ear. No one teased or laughed at him. His friends were aware of the unique attraction between Little Abu and the creatures around him. As he listened to the chirping of the cricket and the *chirr-chirr* of the grasshopper, a long distance away, he could tell whether the sound was made by a male or a female. He had pointed out and explained these differences to his friends over and over. While they strained their ears to listen without success, they never disputed his knowledge. When Little Abu said it was so, that was enough for them.

Nevertheless, the boys were terrified when a passing scorpion, centipede or the vicious and feared red biting ants crawled across Little Abu's bare arm, body or neck, leaving no marks or stings.

Once, a boy named Noah hit a huge, warty toad, which was sunning itself on the dam, with his stick. All the boys laughed except little Abu. "You fool...!" he growled, flying into a rage, hitting the transgressor with his stick. He sulked for the rest of the day, remaining far away from the group, even though he had taken the toad back to the trench and they had seen it swim away. After that incident, his friends were careful not to hit a frog, toad or any creature while he was around. They were frightened of Little Abu's anger.

However, his companions were spellbound when he mimicked the mating call and song of every bird on the island. He knew each bird's identity from its call. It was not uncommon for a thrush or kiskadee, attracted by his call, to sit on his out-stretched arm, trilling and singing as if its chest would burst. Many birds came to his call. And the boys never ceased to be amazed at these performances.

As the afternoon sun started to set, large flocks of showy macaws, parrots and parakeets congregated. Moving from tree to tree, they set up a chattering and squalling. Then upwards they would fly again, colourful in the dazzling light. Joined by flocks of herons, mallards, sea gulls and cranes that nestled on the seashore, they fluttered, picturesque against the sky-blue canvas, plumes bathed in the golden rays of sunset. Together, the birds filled the air with a warlike chattering, screeching, screaming, chirping, chirring. Swirling forward, then backward, then for-ward again, they would race westward, home.

One late afternoon, when the birds were at their loudest, everyone was preparing to leave. In the gathering twilight, the six o'clock bee kept up a tiresome buzzing and the howling mon-keys, invisible to the eye, smote the air with their doleful, impul-sive call, without a break or pause. The boys had already mustered the herds together and were chasing the obedient cattle homeward. Each boy was well aware his cows would instinctively stop off and like homing pigeons enter their own yards.

But the day was far from over. Stealthily, the boys advanced towards the seashore. They were exceptionally quiet, knowing the snapping sound of breaking twigs, the *thud, thud* of footsteps would scare away the prizes. Their faces were a study in pure delight, as giant blue crabs, following the leader in soldier-like files, marched entranced towards the ocean and into the ready and waiting rice bags. Satisfied, the companions moved off without the slightest sound. There was a chance they might discover a turtle or two burrowing in the sand. With a quick flip, the unsuspecting creatures were turned over on their backs. Then hurriedly but carefully, the boys searched for eggs in the sand.

"Listen! What was that unearthly hissing?" With quick, light steps, the friends rushed over to help two of their companions who caught a couple of iguanas, hissing and struggling to get free. The creatures thrashed about wildly, using their tails as whipcords and baring sharp, ugly teeth. But with dexterity the boys tied the tails securely to the iguana's scaly backs, while the captors grinned in triumph. These catches, highly esteemed, were sought after as delicacies.

But Little Abu had not joined the high-spirited group. Like the blue crab, he marched as though entranced over the shifting sand towards the Atlantic Ocean. With ears cocked, body alert, he appeared to be listening. He listened to the dreary, haunting echoes of the wind as it rose and fell, swelling the tide into giant waves, crashing, lashing against each other, furiously rolling into one, only to be spent gradually on the seashore. The boys stared at Little Abu, then from one to the other, speechless, helpless, scared. Little Abu was now standing in the water, knee-deep in the slowly sinking sand, trancelike, muttering. His mutterings grew louder and clearer as he repeated, over and over in singsong, words his friends could not recognize.

Then Little Abu screamed, and immediately the spell he was under seemed to be broken. But only for a moment, as he stumbled out of the water towards them, reeling from side to side.

"You hear...!" he cried out. It was more a statement than a question. For a fleeting moment he gazed at his companions, searching their faces, looking into each one's eyes, expectant, as if they could comprehend or divine the significance of his sudden penetration. He stood before them, breathless, chest heaving, then charged past in the direction of home.

The boys stared after Little Abu, stupified, eyeing each other. They had seen his brown face strained with distress, his dark eyes bright with a knowledge that confused them. As he spoke, they too had leaned forward, listening. But no one responded. They dared not reveal their own thoughts. All they heard was the sighing of the wind. They stood there, hesitating, looking bleak and bewildered, eyes following Little Abu, who had already become a trail of dust in the darkness.

That was the last afternoon Little Abu and his companions spent together as boys. It was a time they would remember for the rest of their lives, because of the things they did together, and the unusual event that brought their relationship to a dramatic, if not abrupt, ending. Later that evening, the news spread around the village: Old Abu was dying.

The boys could not explain why Little Abu's absence created such a void in their daily activities. He had little interest in field work. He was eternally drawn to the plants and animals, spending most of his time observing them. Yet, as the boys passed Little Abu's house the very next morning, they gave the signal, but didn't wait for him down the road. As they ambled along, they gazed back every now and then, wistful, though deep in their hearts they knew he would never join them again.

Death hung over the Abus' household for a little more than a week. As was customary, villagers knocked on the Abus' door during this time but were never successful in seeing any one of the family. No one was admitted. No one ever left the house and no fire was lit for days in the kitchen, which stood apart from the house. The villagers started to whisper among themselves. They claimed they recognized Little Abu's mother's muted, mournful wailings and Little Abu's voice above the weakened chants of his father. At times, they gossiped about the eerie and mysterious silences inside the house. A shadow of suspicion and tension hung over the village.

But curiosity whetted the villagers' appetites for more information, so they continued to knock at the Abus'. They left gifts of food and fresh fruit. There was nothing else they could do, so they waited. Then one morning, a villager passed by and saw the flag. Soon it was all over the island: Old Abu was dead! This time, when the villagers called on the Abus, they were welcomed inside and allowed to share in the family's grief.

Sometime afterwards, the people realized Abu was no longer a boy, though he was no more than fifteen years old at the time. "Abu's now head of our family.... He will provide for us!" Abu's mother, plump and half smiling, announced pleasantly to a villager who called. This announcement troubled the villagers. They had kept a respectful distance after the funeral, while still sharing their bounty of fruit and fish.

"But is how they goin' to make out at all?"

"De poor boy is too young...ow, ow!"

"Is not only dat...man, you ain't see de boy is a dreamer!" they whispered, scoffing at the idea among themselves.

These snatches of conversation took place among neighbours whenever Mrs. Abu appeared in the yard, minding the stock or tending the kitchen garden. Then one day, Mrs. Abu went to the village shop a few miles away. She purchased a large quantity of groceries, cotton fabrics and familiar household items, for which she paid with a handsome sovereign. The shopkeeper was amazed! The gold piece overwhelmed him. He nodded his head as he considered the situation. Mrs. Abu was not a regular customer, that was true. She was one of a breed of quiet, thrifty women. Then Old Abu must have had quite a mint tucked away.

Of course! Indeed, it had slipped his memory. Old Abu made a good trade from his bush medicine and chants! Why, at one time or another, many of the villagers, not excluding himself, had cause to visit Old Abu. The old man never took money but accepted gifts: a calf, a lamb or a young goat, even a half bag of rice. And he was careful to keep no more than five or six head of cattle. Cattle always fetched a good price. Real clever...me buddy smart man! The shopkeeper smiled triumphantly while he busied himself, helping Mrs. Abu pack her many purchases in a huge basket, set it on her head and then with characteristic ease and friendliness, he saw her off. By nightfall, the news had spread like wildfire. The whole island was bubbling with excitement, predicting and calculating the Abus' worth.

When the topic was exhausted, the villagers turned to young Abu. They talked, adding new details, giving new dimension to stories about his "bewitchment" of animals. Of course, during the time he was locked in with his father, they knew exactly what went on and elaborated their views on the subject. The fact that no one was allowed to enter the house, while it was reported that the young lad's and his father's feeble chantings were heard, added more fuel to their imaginations. They recounted the unusual things, things such a "little, little" boy had done, which they had seen with their very own eyes! They babbled, hmmed, ahaaed, shook with displeasure, appeared shocked, and the village buzzed.

Then one day, the boy Noah, who had struck the toad, carried his sick little sister, wrapped in a blanket, to see his friend Abu. Noah waited in the outer room while Abu's mother went inside to fetch him. Abu appeared and Noah was amazed at the change in him. Abu was no longer the boy he had known. He was at least a head taller. Reposed, he stood before his friend, magnificent in a long, flowing white robe, hair closely cropped, fingers entwined across his stomach. Abu moved with the same smooth grace, which had seemed womanish and unfavourable when they romped together as boys. Noah, so taken aback by the change, forgot for a moment the rigid bundle in his arms.

"My friend!" Abu greeted them. His voice sounded different to Noah, yet it stirred strong feelings, reminding him of the not too dim past, reflecting confidence, spirit and humility.

"I see you are well...but your little sister, Beatrice?" Abu's words hung in the air, stunning Noah. Abu could not have known her! Even now, the little body was well wrapped because of the fever, and her face was covered, save for a little opening for breathing. It was really incredible. Beatrice, one of fifteen-month-old twins, was difficult to identify. Yet Abu called her name without removing the blanket.

Abu unwrapped the covering, then placed the rigid infant down gently on the pallet bed. The child lay scarcely moving; only the slight heaving of her chest, followed by a weak moan, signalled she was alive.

"You must leave her...maybe two days!" Abu gestured, nodding his head, touching the distended stomach. "My mother and I..."

"No, no...!" gasped Noah in despair, rushing to his sister's bedside. At that moment Beatrice made a low, whining sound, opening her eyes, which were dark and sunken. "What will I tell my mother?" His voice quavered; he wrung his hands in wild panic.

Abu said nothing. He was already soothing the fevered brow with a piece of cotton dipped in a calabash of pleasant-smelling liquid. Noah was in a dilemma. There was no one else to help his sister. Yet he feared leaving her, a mere infant, with this boy who had developed overnight into the mysterious stranger standing before him. Suddenly, it was clear to him what to do.

He backed towards the wall. Whatever happened, he would remain in the room with Beatrice.

"If you trust me...you must go!" Abu spoke softly but his tone, though compassionate, conveyed a command, startling Noah to his feet as he was about to sit down. He wrung his hands, moaning again and again. However, head bent and without a word, he went through the door, thoroughly perplexed.

Mrs. Abu silently closed it behind him.

By the end of the day, the news had spread and people gathered outside the Abus', watchful, sullen and expectant.

"But is why they keep the people's chile atall?"

"Don't ask me, my girl...dat's what I come to find out!"

"Old Abu nefer do that...he used to gi'e you good good medicine an' send you away!"

"Girl, a time he gi'e me something...ah tell you when ah tek it ah was sick sick sick...but since then awright!"

"Is wha' they doing so long...is wha' they keep de people chile for?"

"To carry on with dey rigmarole...what else!"

Talking loudly, they ridiculed, praised and blamed the Abus. They gossiped nonstop until someone shouted, "All you bettah fetch the police!" And everything grew suddenly quiet.

The Abus ignored the disturbance. They continued with what they were doing as if no one was in their front yard. By nightfall, Abu thought half of the village was camped outside his door. He could see the flicker of their bottle lamps through the cracks in the wall, and he had recognized many of his father's visitors, who had stayed over on countless occasions. Their children too were left quite willingly for his parents to care for. At times, he thought the noise would never end. He pondered the sudden opposition, but was indifferent to their protestations. A few more hours and the child would be well.

He was not afraid of the police, and, besides, they were miles away.

"Eh eh...look de police comin'!" Someone shouted. It was the afternoon of the second day. The villagers, quiet from their watch since the day before, eyed each other awkwardly and with unease. The policeman came into the yard. Everyone remained quiet, making way for him to get through. But before he could, the door was opened by Mrs. Abu, who appeared with a blanket folded and draped over her left arm, leading Beatrice with the other.

"Give her plenty young coconut water," Mrs. Abu said to Beatrice's mother and father, who had instinctively moved forward; she hesitated a moment.

"Ma...Ma!" Beatrice called cheerfully as she hurried to her mother's outstretched arms. The mother came forward, eyes downcast, caught her, looked up, embarrassed, to the open door, but Mrs. Abu made a graceful nod, then closed it.

"Look...the chile get better already!" The mob pushed forward to get a better look at Beatrice in her mother's arms.

"She really looking better!"

"She never look so sprightly before!"

"She was always sickly lookin'!"

"The Abus is decent people...Old Abu was good good man, ah don't know what get into all you head foh sen' foh de police!"

"The young man do a very good job...you all should thank de people," a thoughtful villager said loudly. The mob babbled on without shame.

"The police got no right here!"

That did it. Constable Moriah was exasperated more than he was confused, as he pushed his way back through the crowd and stood aside, mopping his brow. He was the one to give up his lunch hour. He had just finished cooking and left the comfortable shelter of the tiny outpost, walked five miles through the broiling midday sun, and for what! He was supposed to question the Abus about the child. The same child who was right before his eyes, unharmed. He looked about to see if he could identify any of the instigators who had crowded into the small outpost, but couldn't recognize any of them, and wished he had taken down a few names. How he disliked writing long statements! The truth was, he disliked police work more!

"Mr. Policeman! Drink this water coconut; it will cool you down." Out of the blue, a woman, head wrapped with a large colourful head-tie, lopped off the top of a coconut, chipped a small hole in it and thrust it at him.

"You all get off these people property," he barked with forced authority, and the crowd began shuffling off.

Early the next morning, Mrs. Abu went out to milk the cow. She discovered, much to her surprise, a pair of ewes tethered in the yard. She stared at the ungainly creatures for a moment. Then, smiling to herself, she placed them with the other stock and went on with her work. She would tell Abu later, but was certain he already knew about it.

After the healing of Beatrice, word about young Abu grew like lush paddy plants. He was openly approved, his authority accepted and he became highly respected. Consequently, his influence extended to people of diverse persuasions and interests.

A few weeks later a farmer, jealous of his wife, ended her life in a savage manner. The neighbours had always gossiped about his unreasonable attitude and deplored his regular assaults. They had heard her cries against his violent abuse and were outraged; but had kept their distance. On the night in question her cries were unbearable, and therefore a report was made to the police. Early the next morning, Constable Moriah appeared on the scene to investigate the matter. The husband invited him in but maintained his wife had left earlier in the morning to catch the first ferry. She had gone to visit her parents on the coastland. Constable Moriah's suspicion was aroused when he noted a baby among a brood of children, all too young to be taken care of by the father. Unsatisfied, the constable questioned the farmer at length, but the man could not explain why his wife had left the baby.

Then the constable talked to the neighbours, who agreed the woman would never leave the children. The policeman checked the ferry and, convinced the woman never left the island, returned with a warrant to search the house and grounds. He went over every inch of the farmer's house and yard, but found nothing. However, fearful the man would disappear, Constable Moriah arrested him.

Because of the murder investigation and the diggings, the police force on the island was strengthened. They needed a body in order to establish a case against the husband. Also, by this time the woman's distressed parents reported they had not seen her. The investigation was now in the hands of an inspector from the coastland.

Constable Moriah was tired of digging. He argued about the time being wasted and made a suggestion that the body was not anywhere around, hinting they might have to let the man go. Cautiously, he proposed they get young Abu's help. The inspector and the rest of the crew were shocked the constable would venture to make a joke out of the investigation. They turned on him with jibes and taunts. He challenged them with what he had heard about Abu, but they took no notice of him.

The search became extensive, spreading to farmlands down in the backdam. The task was impossible and the crew was exhausted. The inspector threw sideways glances at the men as they mumbled, whispering among themselves, sucking their teeth and yawning unabashed. He was uneasy. He knew what was on their minds and later that evening went to see Abu in secret.

"Tomorrow morning at half-past four, meet me on the bridge. I'll be waiting!" Abu greeted the inspector, who gazed at him speechless. How could Abu know? The inspector hadn't said a word!

Next morning, the inspector and his party arrived some time after four to find Abu waiting on the bridge in front of the yard. As they started off, Abu insisted he walk ahead of them. In this manner they walked, Abu twenty yards or more ahead in long flowing robes with the hood covering his head and bare feet.

Abu led the party straight for the backdam. They walked for miles across farms, trenches and dams. The inspector checked his watch at intervals. It was still dark but the men were sweating and tiring. Through rice fields and cane fields they went on a long and arduous journey. By this time the inspector was sure it was a wild goose chase. The men puffed and sweated as they tried to keep up with Abu.

"What dis man tink itis atall? We working hard all day, while he sitting down in the house!"

"I can't understand why he flying like dat and at four in the mornin'!"

"Watch where you goin', man—you nearly trip me up!"

"Jesus, man, I cyna keep up atall!"

"What de hell is this? Some force driving he, man!'

"You notice too...Look at he, man like he foot ain't touching de ground!"

"And he ain't even looking back!"

"This ain't natural, cyna be natural...this man ain't human!"

Baffled by the mysterious figure ahead, the men tramped laboriously behind, fretting and swearing. But Abu never looked back and he moved like the wind.

Suddenly, Abu stopped and would go no farther. Beckoning to the inspector, he pointed, describing a spot ahead on the dam and insisting the men would discover there what they wanted.

The inspector rushed forward, keeping the men at a distance while he looked for the clues Abu spoke about. In an instant, he called excitedly to the men and, pointing to a spot, instructed them to dig. Within minutes of digging, there was a chorus of enthusiastic cries. The men had found the body, the search was over.

Jubilant, the inspector called loudly, summoning Abu. Getting no response, he hurried forward with expressions of praise. He stared ahead, but Abu was nowhere around. He gazed into the distance. Abu could not have gone far. In excitement, the inspector ran down the dam until he was out of breath, then stopped and took in stretches of the dam as far as the eye could see.

Abu had disappeared completely.

....

Many people continue to use bush medicine to this day. What began as a matter of survival became an indispensable part of a culture. The same is true for other West Indian territories.

Afua Cooper

And I Remember

And I remember
standing
in the churchyard on Wesleyan Hill
standing and looking down on the plains
that stretch before me
like a wide green carpet
the plains full with sugar cane and rice
the plains that lead to the sea

And I remember
walking
as a little girl to school
on the savannahs of Westmoreland
walking from our hillbound village
walking along steep hillsides
walking carefully so as not to trip and plunge
walking into the valley

And I remember
running
to school on the road that cuts into the green carpet
running past laughing waters
running to school that rose like a concrete castle
out of my carpet of green
running with a golden Westmoreland breeze

And I remember
breathing
the smell of the earth plowed by rain and tractors
breathing the scent of freshly cut cane
breathing the scent of rice plants as they send
their roots into the soft mud
Yes, and I remember
thinking
this is mine this is mine
this sweetness of mountains
valleys
rivers
and plains
is mine
mine
mine

Memories Have Tongue

My granny say she have a bad memory when I ask her to tell
me some of her life
say she can't remember much but
she did remember the 1910 storm and how dem house blow down
an dey had to go live with her granny down bottom house
Say she have a bad memory, but she remember
that when her husband died, both of them were thirty,
she had three little children, one in her womb,
one in her arms, one at her frocktail. She remember when
they bury him how the earth buss up under her foot
and her heart bruk inside
that when the baby born she had no milk
her breasts refused to yield.
She remember how she wanted her daughter to grow up and be
a postmistress but the daughter died at an early age
she point to the croton-covered grave at the bottom of the
yard. Say her memory bad, but she remember
1938
Frome
the riot
Busta
Manley
but what she memba most of all is that a pregnant woman,
one of the protesters, was shot an' killed by soldiers.
Say she old now her brains gathering water
but she remember
that she liked dancing as a young woman
and yellow was her favourite colour. She remember
too that it was her husband's father who asked

for her hand. The Parents sat in the hall and discussed
the matter. Her father finally concluded that her man was
an honourable person and so gave his consent.
Her memory bad but she remember
on her wedding day how some of her relatives
nearly eat off all the food. It was all right though, she
said, I was too nervous to eat anyway.

....

In 1938, workers all over the island of Jamaica struck and demonstrated
against deplorable working and living conditions. One of the centres of
these activities was Frome Estate in Westmoreland.

   When the colonial militia was called in to put down the Frome demon-
strations, the militia killed four people. Alexander Bustamante and Norman
Manley were labour and political activists who led the people, and later
became leaders of the country.

Lovetalk

My love enfolds you
my love encircles you
I am the river from which all sweetness flows

My breasts your milkpots
from which you refuse to be weaned
my navel, your centre

You smell my particular smell
and your whole self begins to quiver
I am the tree of life
the giver of your knowledge

You want to remain for ever
in the shadow of my moonglow
to taste its essence
and wonder at its sweetness
I am the river from which all good things flow

Cyril Dabydeen

Phoenix

This bird,
alighting

On blacksage brush
when I fired—

The entire forest
ablaze...

Feathers floating
in the wind—

Leaves scattering
like ash.

Swarthier than ever,
skin burning—

Closer to the ground,
as I experience

Birdsong and wail...
such rememberances

In the night,
flesh of fire,

The tropical wind
patterning

A life—
moulding the sun,

Singeing the years.

Multiculturalism

I continue to sing of other loves,
Places...moments when I am furious;
When you are pale and I am strong—
As we come one to another.

The ethnics at our door
Malingering with heritage,
My solid breath—like stones breaking;
At a railway station making much ado about much,
This boulder and Rocky Mountain,

CPR heaving with a head tax
As I am Chinese in a crowd,
Japanese at the camps,
It is also World War II.
Panting, I am out of breath.

So I keep on talking
With blood coursing through my veins,
The heart's call for employment equity,
The rhapsody of police shootings in Toronto,
This gathering of the stars one by one, codifying them
And calling them planets, one country, really...

Or galaxies of province after province,
A distinct society too:
Québec or Newfoundland; the Territories...
How far we make a map out of our solitudes
As we are still Europe, Asia,
Africa; and the Aborigine in me
Suggests love above all else—
The bear's configuration in the sky;
Other places, events; a turbanned RCMP,
These miracles—

My heritage and quest, heart throbbing;
Voices telling me how much I love you.
YOU LOVE ME; and we're always springing surprises,
Like vandalism at a Jewish cemetery
Or Nelson Mandela's visit to Ottawa
As I raise a banner high on Parliament Hill
Crying "Welcome!"—we are, you are—
OH CANADA!

I am not

1

i am not West Indian
i am not—
let me tell you again and again
let Lamming and Selvon talk of places
            too distant from me;
let me also recover and seethe
& shout with a false tongue
if I must—
that i am here
nowhere else

let me also conjure up other places
as i cry out that all cities are the same,
rivers, seas, oceans—
how they swell or surrender
            at the same source

2

i breathe in the new soil
engorging myself with wind,
yet flaccid—

i inhale the odour
of rice paddy
cane leaves in the sun
& birds blacker than the familiar vulture
circling my father's house
with a vague promise

            amidst other voices
i come together with you,
crying out
that there are hinterlands,
other terrain

3

we fashion new boundaries
            and still i do not know,
i do not know,
in the cold, this heat
of the insides—
wetness at the corners of the mouth

skin grown lighter,
& once the giant lake,
foamy whiteness of my Ottawa river—
            now Mohawk or Algonquin...
whither Carib or Arawak?

i breathe harder
with my many selves,
            turning back

Lawrence Hill

So What Are You, Anyway?

Carole settles in Seat 12A, beside the window, puts her doll
on a vacant seat and snaps open her purse. She holds up a
mirror. She looks into her own dark eyes. She examines her
handful of freckles, which are tiny ink spots dotting her cheeks.
She checks for pimples, but finds none. Only the clear complex-
ion that her father sometimes calls "milk milk milk milk choco-
late" as he burrows into her neck with kisses.

"This is yours, I believe." A big man with a sunburnt face is
holding her doll upside down.

"May I have her, please?" Carole says.

He turns the doll right side up. "A black doll! I never saw
such a thing!"

"Her name's Amy. May I have her, please?"

"Henry Norton!" cries the man's wife. "Give that doll back
this instant!"

Carole tucks the doll close to the window.

The man sits beside Carole. The woman takes the aisle seat.

"Don't mind him," the woman says, leaning towards Carole.

"By the way, I'm Betty Norton, and he's my husband, Henry."

The man next to Carole hogs the armrest. His feet sprawl onto her side. And he keeps looking at her.

The stewardess passes by, checking seat belts. "Everything okay?"

"May I go to the bathroom?" Carole asks.

"Do you think you could wait? We're about to take off."

"Okay."

Carole looks out the window, sees the Toronto airport buildings fall behind and wonders if her parents are watching. Say goodbye, she instructs Amy, waving the doll's hand, say goodbye to Mom and Dad. The engines charge to life. Her seat hums. They taxi down the runway. She feels a hollowness in her stomach when they lift into the air. Her ears plug and stay that way until the plane levels out over pillows of cotton. They burn as bright as the sun. So that is what the other side of clouds look like!

"Excuse me. *Excuse me!*" The man is talking to her. "You can go to the bathroom now, you know."

"No, that's all right," Carole says.

"Travelling all alone, are you?"

Carole swallows with difficulty.

"Where do you live?" he asks.

"Don Mills."

"Oh, really?" he says. "Were you born there?"

"Yes."

"And your parents?"

"My mother was born in Chicago and my father was born in Tucson."

"And you're going to visit your grandparents?"

She nods.

"And your parents let you travel alone!"

"It's only an airplane! And I'm a big girl."

The man lowers the back of his seat, chuckling. He whispers to his wife. "No!" Carole hears her whisper back, "*You* ask her!"

Carole yawns, holds Amy's hand and goes to sleep. The clinking of silverware wakens her, but she hears the man and woman talking about her, so she keeps her eyes shut.

"I don't know, Henry," says the woman. "Don't ask me. Ask *her*."

"I'm kind of curious," he says. "Aren't you?"

Carole can't make out the woman's answer. But then she hears her say:

"I just can't see it. It's not fair to children. I don't mind them mixed, but the world isn't ready for it. They're neither one thing nor the other. Henry, wake that child and see if she wants to eat."

When the man taps her shoulder, Carole opens her eyes. "I have to go to the bathroom," she says.

"But they're going to serve the meal," the man says.

"Henry! If she wants out, let her out. She's only a child."

Carole grimaces. She is definitely not a child. She is a young lady! She can identify Drambuie, Kahlua, and Grand Marnier by smell!

Once in the aisle, Carole realizes that she has forgotten Amy.

Henry Norton hands her the doll. "There you go. And don't fall out of the plane, now. There's a big hole down by the toilet."

"There is not!" Carole says. "There isn't any such thing!" She heads down the aisle with an eye out just in case there is a hole, after all.

Coming out of the toilet, Carole finds the stewardess. "Excuse me, miss. Could I sit somewhere else?"

The woman frowns. "Why?"

"I don't like the window."

"Is that it? Is that the only reason?"

"Well...yes."

"I'm sorry, but we don't have time to move you now. We're serving a meal. Ask me later, if you like."

After Carole had eaten and had her tray taken and been served a hot face towel, the man says: "What *are* you, anyway? My wife and I were wondering."

Carole blinks, sees the man's clear blue eyes and drops her head.

"What do you mean?" she says.

"You know, what are you? What race?"

Carole's mouth drops. Race? What is that? She doesn't understand. Yet she senses that the man is asking a bad question. It is as if he is asking her something dirty, or touching her in a bad place. She wishes her Mom and Dad were there. They could tell her what "race" meant.

"That doll of yours is black," Henry Norton says. "That's a Negro doll. That's race. Negro. What's your race?"

The question still confuses her.

"Put it this way," the man says. "What is your father?"

The question baffles her. What is her father? He is her Dad! He is her Dad and every Sunday morning he makes pancakes for the whole family and lets Carole pour hot syrup on them and afterwards he sits her on his lap and tells stories.

Mrs. Norton leans towards Carole. "Say you had a colouring book. What colour would you make your Dad?"

"I never use just one colour."

"Okay. What colour would you make his face?"

"Brown."

"And your mother?"

Carole imagines a blank page. What would she put in her

mother's face? She has to put something in there. She can't just leave it blank. "I don't know."

"Sure you do," Mrs. Norton says. "How would you colour your mother's face?"

"Yellow."

Carole sees Mr. and Mrs. Norton look at each other.

"Is your mother Chinese?" Mrs. Norton asks.

"No."

"Are you sure you'd colour her yellow?"

"No."

"What else might you colour her?"

What else? Carole feels ashamed at her stupidity. A tear races down her cheek. "Red," she says, finally.

"Red! You can't colour a face red! Is your mother white? Is she like me? Her face! Is it the same colour as mine?"

"Yes."

"And your father's brown?"

Carole nods.

"When you say brown, do you mean he is a Negro?"

"Yes." Of course her father is a Negro. If Mrs. Norton wanted to know all along if her Dad was a Negro, why didn't she just ask?

"So you're mixed?" Mrs. Norton says. "You're a mulatto!"

Carole's lip quivers. What is mulatto? Why do they keep asking her what she is? She isn't anything!

"So is that it? You're a mulatto? You know what a mulatto is, don't you? Haven't your parents taught you that word?"

Approaching with a cart of juice, the stewardess looks up and smiles at Carole. That gives her a rush of courage.

"Leave me alone!" she screams at Mrs. Norton.

Passengers stare. The stewardess spills a drink. Mrs. Norton sits back hard in her seat, her hands raised, fingers spread. Carole sees people watching.

"Why do you keep asking me if my Dad is Negro? Yes, he's a Negro! Okay? OKAY? Negro Negro Negro!"

"Calm down," Mrs. Norton says, reaching over.

"Don't touch her," the stewardess says.

"Who are these people?" someone says from across the aisle. "Imagine, talking to a child like that, and in 1970!"

One woman sitting in front of Carole stands up and turns around.

"Would you like to come and sit with me, little girl?"

"No!" Carole shouts. "I don't like all these questions. She keeps asking me how I would colour my parents in a colouring book! Why do you keep asking me that?"

Mrs. Norton pleads with Carole to stop.

"How would you like it if that happened to you?" Carole says. "So what are you, anyway? What are your parents? How would you colour them? Well, I don't care! I don't even care!"

"How would you like to come and sit with me?" the stewardess says, smiling. "I'll make you a special drink. Have you ever had a Shirley Temple?"

Carole nods enthusiastically. Already she feels better. Clutching Amy, she passes by the Nortons, who swing their legs to let her out.

"My God," Carole hears Mrs. Norton tell her husband, "talk about sensitive."

George Elliott Clarke

Casualties
January 16, 1991

Snow annihilates all beauty
this merciless January.
A white blitzkrieg, Klan—cruel,
arsons and obliterates.

Piercing lies numb us to pain.
Nerves and words fail so we
can't feel agony or passion,
so we can't flinch or cry,

when we spy blurred children's
charred bodies protruding
from the smoking rubble
of statistics or see a man

stumbling in a blizzard
of bullets. Everything is
normal, absurdly normal.
We see, as if through a snow-

storm, darkly. Reporters
rat-a-tat-tat tactics,
stratagems. Missiles bristle
behind newspaper lines.

Our minds chill; we weather
the storm, huddle in dreams.
Exposed, though, a woman,
lashed by lightning, repents

of her flesh, becomes a living
X-ray, "collateral damage."
The first casualty of war
is language.

April in Paris

    Elms etch against the watercolour sky.
I exult in sprays of green—vines and leaves
Leaping up walls, occupying *les rues*.
Africans on the white steps of Sacre Coeur
Sell gold tinted by barter and banter;
They curry a spicy callaloo
Of currencies into francs. The pigeons are
Up to no good, dreaming of July's heat.
Une beauté peels a newspaper from cool
And steady wind. We are home in April.
The pigeons startle at my too-loud thought
And wheel into the pale heaven. Verdant

Messieurs wielding long brooms, sweep shit—
And old manuscripts—from the cobblestones.
　　I wander among the graves of poets,
Stalk inspiration with a loaded pen,
And collect bunches of fresh, cold lilies.
I keep thinking of you, so, so lovely,
Rambling the ramparts of the Citadel
Of Quebec. I want to drape you in silks,
Array you in beautiful, gaudy flags,
But you've kept me drifting all of this time.
　　If you will offer me another home—
A balcony where I may type this poem,
I will bring you wine and albescent honey.
I will bring you kisses of albescent honey.
I'll name you with the most beautiful nouns:
Carnation, orchid, rose, iris, trillium, anemone.

April 19, 19__

　　He was falling apart under the pressure of love;
his blood gelled slowly into honey:
nectar was accumulating in his veins.
Becoming fierce and fiercer for her, his measures
broke up sonnets because they couldn't accommodate
the immense pleasure of her kiss.
　　Troubadours and toreadors sang of her all night
so he couldn't sleep. Her name quarried *corrida*
and *querida*. She seemed to have been born in silk,
a liquid, icy fire that chilled her skin,

inciting her nerves to gasp at the caress.
Her kisses were rain upon his face.
    He brought her lilies and the bluesiest
albas ever strummed by a Nova Scotian,
yielding their private language to a public form,
because of the night she lay beside him
and the day they lolled in apple blossoms.
They were guilty of unspeakable love.
    There was the beginning and that only:
the first poem that made her gasp; the first embrace
that made him echo a millennium of songs
By entombed, regretful poets who wished
They had known lips as full and soft as hers.
Their love survives now only in this poem.

Marina: The Love Song of Lee Harvey Oswald

    Here are some early narcissus for your blue eyes,
Marina Prusakova.
Let's mose beside the River Minsk—you, nineteen and perfect,
And I just twenty-one.
Look, in still life, Father Lenin smiles upon us.
Take these blue plums and some hot, black tea.
    I've scribbled in my Historic Diary
About the workers's future—sunlight sifting
Through birch branches and hydroelectric towers,
Silvering everything, everything.
I promise you we'll blind history!

Taste these sweet plums, Marina.
    Let's dawdle in doorways while the snow mills:
This world is like a coming storm.
Peasants will throw flowers when our steamer aways,
Silver narcissus petals snow through air,
When we embark for glimmering America
To become its shining President and First Lady.

To Milton Acorn

    Death's plain idiocy, maker. There's no
Music in it, only suspires of rain
And sighs of dumb, worm-ravished earth. Naive
Carpenter, where's your voice now that once sang
Of love and anger in jack-pine meters
That couldn't be planed to fit pre-fab verse?
    You were our Miltonic, Atlantic Lear,
A raging, white-bearded, word-weathered bard,
Who howled against the liars' legislatures.
How can I speak of you?
    I break!
I break from the tension of the iambic line.
    Craftsman, does your voice cry through crows
Or does the grave open its mouth and sing?

April 3–4, 1968

A century of rain crashes home in night,
Dark richness. He sojourns through wet lightning
To the church to sing his death. He feels it
Like sparks, something blazing the shrouded air.
He unveils the bright Bible in his head;
Sudden lightning enraptures the black church.
To the pulpit he rises, thundering
Justice, Jesus, and John, because God has
Shown him The Promised Land; his voice crackles,
"I've been to the mountaintop." The next day,
After the rain, he steps into the cool
Evening, into the cool, April evening.
    Andy dreams he hears an engine crackle.
Ralph jumps "instinctively," then turns, then turns,
And sees King, arms outstretched, the blood crashing
From the hole the bullet's punched through his neck.

Austin Clarke

Letter of the Law of Black

Edgehill House,
Edgehill Road,
Edgehill Gap,
Edgehill Lane,
Edgehill Hill,
Barbados

My dear only Son,

I take up my pen in hand to send you these salutations, hoping that the reaches of them will find you in a perfect state of good health, as they leave me feeling fairly well, at present.

I am telling you this now, at this rather late time, because when you left Barbados to go away, there was too much emotion in the air to talk to you and make sense. Most of the things said were what I call emotion; and all that emotion was good for someone as young as you, taking up a journey in life, to a country which is strange to you, although you were born there. The emotion itself was not complete, was not real emotion, and it rang a bit empty because the one person who could have made the rafters ring for joy, that you, her child, were going to a place where she had so many happy years, was not there. Then was not the time. Then was not the occasion to bring back memories whose only meaning and point in bringing them up would have demanded the bringing up also of the tragedy which defines those memories of happiness. Your mother.

I waited also because I wanted to be sure that you got through your first year in Toronto. The first year is always the hardest. It is the happiest and the saddest. You are free from whatever responsibilities being at home assumes you should carry; and you are alone in a new freedom; and very often you need someone to help you confine yourself within that very freedom. And if I remember correctly, from my own days at Trinity College, the first year demands complete attention to details that prove later to be a complete waste of time. You have to watch your allowance and be a banker; an economist; an investor; and, worst of all, a hoarder. God help you that you do not, like me, have to be a hoarder. You see a shirt for ten dollars, and you buy it because you think it is a saving: but, the next day, you pass a shop window and you see the same shirt, on sale, for half the price. And being new, you do not know and would never think that you could take the ten-dollar shirt off your back, and put it in a nice parcel, and return it, because you could say, had you learned, "This shirt is too small for me."

Is Stollery's Emporium for Men still at the intersection of Bloor and Yonge streets? I spent many dollars and more hours in that store, getting the wrong advice and the proper fit from the male clerks, than I can recount. Their shirts are not bad. But the best ones I wore, and still have some of, were obtained either at the Annual Jewish Sale of clothes in the

Exhibition Gardens down at the Ex, or at a second-hand establishment named the Royal Ex-Toggery, near the Anglo-Saxon residential district of Rosedale. So, you see, I took the best—the best of second-hand!—from the best of both Toronto worlds, at the time. I am talking about the fifties. Now, as I have been reading from the clippings you have sent down, the place is a virtual potpourri of nationalities and something called multiculturalisms.

I noticed the titles of your small but well-chosen library of books. I was pleased to see that although you read the Classics, you still had time besides Latin and Greek for good literature. You should, whilst you are there and during the term breaks, look at the Russians, especially Pushkin. You know, he was one of us! By that I mean a colonial man, more than I mean the obvious: that he was black. Even in your position of being in a minority amongst all this multiculturalism, through colour, in a country like Canada, whose immigration policy was officially white up until 1950, the fact of being a colonial—you young intellectuals would say "post-colonial" or "neo-colonial," but I am old, and old-fashioned, and I say colonial—the colonial is the fact that transcends blackness. Blackness may change when you are amongst all black students; or it may change when you are in the company of good white people. (Have you had the chance to look up Mr. Avrom Lampert yet, as I have asked you to do, and pay him your respects? He was extremely kind to me, and most helpful. I have eaten more bagels and lackeyes, or lat-kees—do you spell it so?—in his home during my time in Toronto, than I have eaten flying fish and peas and jerk pork. I hope he is still in the quick. I still owe him the fifty dollars he lent me, thirty years ago, to pay a bill. Shirts, I think. Definitely, pay him my respects. But use your discretion in paying him that old obligation.)

You should browse through some Russian literature. In addition to Pushkin, I would think that Dostoyevski's *Crime and Punishment* would be worthwhile.

One winter, when I was flat on my back with fever, indisposed through health, in a small attic room on College Street near where the main Public Library used to be, I took out and read *Crime and Punishment* in two days of delirium and high temperature. I got worse. They rushed me to the Toronto General Hospital, they meaning two Canadian students who rented rooms that summer in the same house. Dr. Guile, the physician who saw me in Emergency, just smiled and told me to get a bottle of Gordon's Dry Gin. I had told him of Dostoyevski. I hope you won't have that kind of relapse when you seek to broaden your literary horizons. If you were to read *Das Kapital* or *The Communist Manifesto*, even though you were reading for your degree in Political Science and Economics, polly-si-and-ec, they will say you are a communist. You may, if you read these two ideologies, have to hide their tolerance under your academic gown. But if you are seen reading Pushkin, or Dostoyevski or Tolstoy, they will say you are an intellectual. Even if they called you a colonial intellectual, it would be different. You would be more dangerous to them; and they would not be able to despise, or, worse still, ignore, your presence.

Who are these "they"? "They" are all the unmentionable spies, the unnameable people, people who watch you when you do not know they're watching you, when you do not feel they are, or should; and who take it upon themselves to be your sponsors. Beware of sponsors. Beware of liberals. Beware of patronage. Beware of fools.

One day, Kay called me. She was crying. Her fiancé had met a Canadian woman, much older than she, and older than he, who had a child, nine years old. You know who Kay is. He told his colleagues in the Sociology of Violence As It Affects course that he was going to marry this Canadian girl. And he did. And Kay killed herself. But before she killed herself, he never apologized to her. Never called. Never wrote a letter to avoid breach of promise. Never sent a message. Was not mortified by the mortification of Breacher of Promise, or by the violence Kay's stepfather had promised him as a new wedding gift, or by the violent sociology of the jilter.

The church had been booked, she said. The reception, in a rec room—what a doleful term! A rec...could it be a wrecked room?—was booked for the reception, she said. Flowers were ordered, she said. Her girlfriends at the bank, all tellers, and of lies, presumably, were invited, she said; and had bought their wedding dresses, she said. Everything was arranged, she said. The "wrecked" room was vacuumed twice by the superintendent of the apartment building, she said. It was situated in a dreary district of Toronto, where there were five factories and one slaughterhouse, for cows and for pigs.

I don't know why and how I got started on Kay. But having begun, you shall hear the end of that part of my life. I do intend, however, that the end of my life shall be slightly postponed. At seventy-one, I intend, as I have said before you left Barbados, to begin at Genesis, and word-for-work, word-for-worm, work my way through until I reach Revelation and the Concordance. Another poetical word. I feel I have reached concordance with you, my son, in the writing of this letter, at this stage; for after Hitler has been fed his rice and fishheads—hoping no bones are caught in his swallow pipe!—and I have read a few chapters of Exodus, I shall retire for the night, and join you again, soon, in a concordance of love and of deep nostalgia. I hope to complete both: this letter, and the Good Book; and I wonder which of the three remaining duties of my remaining days shall have been dispatched first? The Good Book? The letter? Or my life?

The feelings which I have been expressing to you, and which I have been expressing particularly with more emotion and honesty, are taking hold of me; because all of a sudden, you are not here, not here in this big old house, whose emptiness echoes as if it were a rock quarry, and I myself dynamiting coral stone. It is an old house. And it is larger, too large for one man who spends almost every hour of the day and night inside it, alone. But it is a happy house. A warm house. A museum of memories and events and things which have been ourselves and our past and our aspirations. Your absence gives me the joyful opportunity both to view these things and to rearrange them. Your absence, I hope, is merely temporary—four years of study in that city which, at this time of year, must be forgetting the life-fulness of summer. I was talking about feelings. Yes, these new feelings which I must be expressing to you with a vengeance you had not known before, are feelings more characteristic of a mother; a woman who follows her child into another land with words of love and of reminiscence. And in the case of most women, this kind of love and reminiscence need not be pure love. It could be a transmitting of the cord of birth, the maternal cord, the umbilical restriction that reminds the child, the daughter, that she owes an unpayable debt for being born. It is important that you understand. I do not wish you to miscalculate my motives, even if they are devious.

I have, and I probably transmit, feelings to you that state I am not only your old, irreverent father, but am behaving as if there were a piece of the woman, the mother, inside my advice and words. And I hope that, as a wise man, with the blood of your dead mother's veins inside you, an Edgehill, that you will disregard all the advice I have been giving you, because I am speaking a different language, and breathing in a different air. Disregard it as a modus vivendi: but regard it as a piece of history, to be used as a comparison. Having now absolved you from all filial encumbrances of the mind, let me now incarcerate you immediately for your choice of a philosophical position which is not valid, or tenable, precisely because, as I have said earlier, you have not assumed that there was a history before your time at Trinity College.

You said you wrote a paper on the British Constitution, and your professor gave you a B. You said you showed your paper to a Canadian friend, and he asked you to let him use it as his own submission. In the same course, you said. To the same professor, you said. The same length, you said. The identical paper, you said. The only change in the paper, you said, was that your Canadian friend put his name, a name different from yours, on the paper. You said all these things. These are the facts of the case. And your Canadian friend got an A for the paper, you said. And you ask me now, if this is not racial discrimination, or bigotry, or unfairness? It is not so much your shock that it happened, and to you, as that there was no explanation, no regret, no forgiveness from anyone, when you pointed it out to the two of them.

I myself am shocked that you would have confronted the professor with his own bigotry. I am also shocked that you expected, and did not get, an apology from him. You seem to feel that all these incidents of bad manners, all these expressions of a lower-class, peasant syndrome and mentality, have begun with your presence at Trinity College, and that Trinity College is above that rawness of disposition. Had you an eye to history, to the reality and the logic, that other black men before you have passed through Trinity College, you would not now be so smitten by your paltry experience. Have you ever thought of a day in their lives, in the year 1931?

You are, in spite of the black American Ralph Ellison, who would claim that you are "invisible," you are rather outstanding and conspicuous, and as they say, nowadays, through that thing called multiculturalism, most visible. You are also a conscience. And you should also know that part of our make-up, of our psyche, is hidden, is dark, is criminal, is Christian, is pure, is degenerate and is beautiful.

There was a group of West Indians at a place in Montreal, a second-rate place, called Sir George Williams. Montreal, as you know, and in spite of what you may be hearing amongst the Anglophones at Trinity College, is essentially a French city. Why did I say this, when I am really speaking about the West Indians, and a bigoted professor of Biology, and not about the culture of the place? Anyhow. The West Indians protested. And the administration at Sir George, which had become during these protests a most determinedly third-rate institution, ignored their pleas. The West Indians then held a demonstration. They held it in a room where there was a computer. I never could understand that computer. Why did they not demonstrate in the department of Biology? Or at the professor's home? In my estimation, it would have been better to have done one or the other. However, the computer was damaged. Allegedly damaged by the West Indians, they said. The West Indians were arrested. The West Indians were charged. The West Indians were later sentenced. To various prisons. And to various prison terms. One of them is now a Senator down here. Another is a Senator up there. Does Trinity College have a computer? Do you wish to be a Senator? Up there? Or down here?

In my own experience at Trinity College, I fought that kind of bigotry, in a humorous manner. When I felt it was in the college, and that I was a victim of it, that I was, as I have said of you, a conscience, I merely copied my paper in Political Science (it was also on the British Constitution!) and on one copy I put the name of a student who I knew was getting the best grades, undeservedly so. I submitted that copy with his name first. I had arranged with this person that he would not submit a paper and spoil my stratagem. He was, moreover, lazy. When the professor had read that paper, and had given him an A, I then submitted the other copy. Of the same paper. But with my name. The professor gave me a B-minus. I took both papers, and without talking to anyone, I reread them to reassure myself that they were identical, word for word. When I was convinced of this, I took the first page with my name on it, and pinned it onto the other pages of the other paper—the professor always wrote his comments and the grade on the last page—and then I asked for an appointment. He registered an A in his book for me; and for the other student, who had by now not submitted a paper at all, he gave an A-minus. I had made certain, however, that this was the last course and the last examination I had to take with this gentleman. He was an Englishman. He spoke with a Cockney accent. He came from Cork. His shirts were always dirty at the neck and at the cuffs. He did not buy them at Stollery's Emporium for Men; and he did not know about the Annual Jewish Sale, or the Royal Ex-Toggery. He didn't even know a latkey from a lackey.

These are not the same sentiments I like to send, in a red-white-and-blue airmail envelope, with a fifty-cent stamp on it, all the way from this island of Barbados to you, up there, buried almost up to your knees in snow; and in hostility. I thank you for sending me the phonograph record by Lionel Richie, *Games People Play*. It is also the title of a book by a man named Toffler. I could never understand why so much attention was given to Toffler's book, which I have not read, and so little to Lionel Richie's song. The Third Symphony of Beethoven's arrived without a scratch or a warp.

Unfortunately, the music that the Government Radio in this place plays is like the voices of the politicians: vulgar. "Games People Play," which I remember dancing to, with Kay, almost every Saturday night at a West Indian calypso club where the notorious civil rights lawyer, Charlie Roach, played guitar, badly, fifty years ago, is still fresh and contemporary in my mind, and very sensual. Is it the same "Games People Play?" If Hitler were a woman, Hitler and I would make a few steps.

It is the kind of music that makes you want to dance with a dog! Timeless. Incidentally, although I do not advocate that you become a Christian, I do insist that you sit in a church at least once a month. But preferably in the Church of England. If you could stumble into a Catholic church, or if you are taken there, choose the best: the old cathedral at the corner of King and Church. Sit inside a church. Listen to the music. Pay less attention to the sermon. The sermon is not meant for you, for us, for our people. But the liturgy and the ritual are artistically rewarding. And so is the liturgical music. So far as Trinity College is concerned, and in case you are hung over and desperate on Saturday nights, and cannot rise for breakfast before the dining hall closes, slip into the Chapel; take a seat in the rear; find the hymn; sing it loudly; but not as if you are the soloist; and before the worms in your unrepentant stomach growl you out of favour amongst the "denines," as we called the Theological students, and amongst the sincere worshippers, who are there because of the breakfast that is served after the collection plate, you may find yourself amongst the blessed—meaning the hungry poor. For the rich would not have risen so early on a Sunday morning; and when they do not rise, instead of oranges and bran flakes and soft honey that is grey in colour and bran bread and bran toast and warm milk and bacon done too hard and soft-boiled eggs, they would rather soothe their constitution with caviar and champagne. If you were here, at Edgehill House, you would be partaking of our Sunday breakfast: crab backs stuffed with pork and champagne. (I found a bottle dated 1943. Dom-Pee.) A pity it is that I cannot fold a crab into this red-white-and-blue air-mail envelope, and send it to you!

"Games People Play" is old. It is also a song that keeps coming back to my ears, and whose emotion will not let me forget the sadness of love spent in Toronto. But I have to begin to scratch my way through Genesis, in this concordance of journey, and watch for the bones in Hitler's supper.

Hoping that the reaches of these few lines have found you with your own concordance,

I remain...

Nigel Darbasie

Winter Stroll in Tipaskan

The schoolyard provides visual relief
yet not without its own clutter.
A large open space covered in snow
packed and cratered under millions of footprints.

In every direction, rows of houses and apartments
rectangular in stucco and aluminum siding
with sloped rooftops shingled brown, grey, black.
Metal chimneys glinting in the sun.

The eye wanders. Sights along crooked fences
studies the thin nakedness of backyard trees.
Then returning to the horizon
is caught unexpectedly
by rounded minarets with arched portals
a crescent moon and star.

The Oracle of Babylon

Tear up this wonderful city
burn it to the ground?
Man, all you crazy yes.
Better out the flambeau
rest the pickaxe and sledgehammer
before somebody damage the place.

What happen, you don't like nice thing?
Look this fancy dining set
you could be eatin from
in yuh split-level luxury home
with swimming pool, up in the Heights.
Then imagine the two-car garage
with Porsche and Mercedes inside.

On a winter's night, step out
in a fur coat sweepin to yuh ankle.
Accent with some gold chain
a scatter of diamonds.
But don't tell nobody
we love glitter just like white folks.
And when they roll their eye
in yuh purse or wallet
is fifty-dollar bills
padding a line-up of credit card.
Now that's a good feeling.

Bring down Western society?
Well is book learnin you go need
to convert these millions of worshippers.
And don't let me hear
all you break some showcase on mainstreet.
Throw a big TV on yuh back
run up the road
call that a cultural revolution.

Conceiving the Stranger

First define the tribal self
in skin colour, language
religion, culture.
Add to that
boundaries
of nation, city
village or street.
And there you are:
out of place
a foreigner
the strange other
a moving violation
of tribal differences.

Rozena Maart

Conceptualizing the Immaculate

It was at this occasion when Sarah thought it appropriate to announce her dissatisfaction with the priest. She proceeded with no paper in her hand, unlike the many attendants, to voice what might be the most dissatisfying news for the whole committee. She ruffled her skirt and walked towards the door, where several women were gathering to plan the upcoming Sunday school festival. Many mothers complained about Father John's methods of organizing, and others objected to his somewhat abusive manner. Looking ruffled, she thought, may cause the women to pay her some attention. Father John had been away and the determined twelve-year-old female child was more than pleased about his absence. She paced the wooden floor, sometimes glancing at the ceiling and looking for places where she had previously hidden and gathered her strength.

Before approaching the door, she watched and touched the wooden image of Mary, still rigid and in place in the Nativity scene. Mary's makers had ensured that she was gracefully endowed with fine features: her lips slim and silent, her eyes indirect and wondering, her expression angelic, with an air of gracefulness that only a painful heart like Sarah's could erase. Sarah did not know that the colour of the wood had been selected by Father John. He, the priest fulfilling his mission, had selected the carvings because, surely, he could not allow his Nova Scotian Natives to ever think that Mary was remotely as dark as the wood suggested. The carvings were smooth. They had an air about them, a sense of superiority, as if placing them in the church endowed them with biblical powers.

Caught between the almost seductive Mary and her decision to disclose her own immaculate conception, Sarah wondered whether her testimony would be so well received: whether others would bow before her and praise her and the child she was to bring forth into her black world. Mesmerized by Mary's presence, Sarah stared at the statue in front of her with hypnotic fervour. Suddenly, it seemed alive. She caressed Mary's arms and touched her erect wooden breasts, fondling them the way she had had her own protruding nippled flesh fondled by both her biological father and Father John. They had started touching her at the same time. When, she could hardly remember.

Then she anxiously started searching the wooden Mary, looking for an expected part that she had waited and wanted to touch. She searched without hesitation beneath the cloth that was Mary's dress and opened Mary's rigid wooden legs. "It's not here," she gasped. "It's not here." She searched again, turning Mary upside down in the hope that what she was looking for may have gone somewhere else. "There is no vagina," she whispered. "No vagina." Sarah found not one trace that Mary had ever borne a child.

The infuriated young female child undid her skirt and searched for the large silver pin that kept her clothing together. Her first entry was fierce. And, like her own first entry, there was no foreplay, no preparation, only a few stolen moments to ease the need for unlawful, immediate, sexual gratification. She pierced and cursed and swore and bled as she vaginized the Mother of Jesus. She stuck her pricked fingers deep into the wooden image thousands had observed. As she panted and carved and panted and nail-scratched Mary a vagina, the tears clouded her vision of a Nativity that was of no relation to her as a Native. Her fingers bled all over Mary until the statue was covered in blood and tears, the fluids of her womanhood. As she dug and carved anxiously, Mary's body disappeared into the ground and chips of wood splintered their way onto the floor and her face. Sarah's skirt was hanging loosely about her straight-waisted, protruding stomach. Finally, she sighed in exultation. The perfect image of Mary had been destroyed. Mary now had a vagina, but she was of no use to the packaged scene that bore the memory of the birth of Jesus and signalled the sacrifices of millions of people, who had to abdicate all sense of inner power and submit to Christianity for the sake of survival.

Sarah stared long and hard at the door to the meeting room and wondered whether anyone had heard her crying. The door stayed shut and Sarah remained crouched on the wooden floor, sucking at her bloody fingers. She was familiar with the taste, although this time she clenched her hands with pleasure. These stains she had sustained during a fight with Mary, unlike other times when she had sucked her blood-stained fingers in the hope of swallowing the memories. On the kitchen floor of her home and the kitchen floor of the rectory, she had crouched and sucked the flesh she wore like a stamp. Which one was it first? she thought almost aloud, and jolted into an upright position as she heard a door slam behind her. She crept under the rows of wooden pews and lay watching Mary, listening to Father John's bold biblical steps and observing his strides of confidence as he entered the church. Sarah lay silent and in pain, clenching both her hands, folding them helplessly into her mouth. Two more steps and he'll see me, she thought.

Father John had played hide-and-seek before, and when he had found his unwilling hider, he had ejaculated almost immediately, as though all his libidinous desires were centred on the search. Sarah was his prize. It was late one afternoon after the girls' choir had returned from an outing in the woods when Father John had first started playing his games. It was not unusual for him to request that Sarah stay behind. The choir outings were a joy to Sarah because they were a time for her to be with female children her own age. She laughed and giggled as they did, imitating the gestures that her father silenced, indulging in stories and jokes about boys who wanted peeks under their dresses, until her face hardened when she learned that the girlish desires of her peers, practised in this atmosphere of fantasy and comfort, were already a reality for her. To her peers Sarah was a respected female child who had earned the reputation of an honorary adult. Motherless since the tender age of seven, she took care of her father and four brothers, each delighting in motherly attention from a child who needed it herself so dearly. At breakfast, she prepared three different cereals and poured endless cups of tea, as each brother demonstrated his desire to have his cup filled and dear old father gestured with stares, moving his eyes in the direction of what he desired. His boots were securely tied and his face was patted as Sarah lifted herself from the ground, just as her mother used to do. The four boys had their sandwiches wrapped in particular ways so that each could identify which was his. By the time Sarah was ten years old, she had managed to run a house without ever knowing the joy of learning to read a book. Sarah's admiration of books gave Father John many clues. He knew that she cherished the unknown. Father John would motion for her from the desk to his lap—each time teaching Sarah about his own misguided and deceitful desires. His long black robe twirled itself around him more times than he deserved. It embarrassed him with righteousness and hid his fondling abusive hands, which covered every detail of Sarah's black body. It camouflaged a priest who hid his carnal desires and performed them regularly upon an unwilling child.

One day, Father John overheard the giggling conversation of the girls and forbade it, warning that it stole time away from God's work: that girls ought to be girls and give their souls and hearts to the Lord, who would cleanse them and keep them protected from the evils of the devil. As he gripped her hand, Father John showed Sarah that he favoured her. Her peers watched with envy as Father John explained to Sarah how the cow had given birth to the calf. She knew that something was already growing inside her and soon her calf would want to leave too. That day, she remained silent on the bus and protested not a word when her father mounted her upon his bed that same evening, but listened to the crying calf and the swaying trees vomiting inside her stomach.

Lying silently under the pews, Sarah watched the boots of Father John, cursing the moment of his entry. She wondered if he could smell her, as he had complained on occasion, and offered holy waters to clean her soiled and unbathed parts. But no. Father John checked his wristwatch and proceeded into the meeting room, where disapproving voices announced his arrival. He commanded the attention of the women and held it for a long time. Sarah rolled over to the end of the pew and lifted herself without erasing the traces of her presence. She remained silent as she realized the fear of the women she so admired. It was clear where their commitments lay. Their Christian duty had forbidden them to challenge the man who preached the gospel of obedience. To Sarah, it marked a moment of defeat. It was clear to her that she could no longer rely on their goodwill. The tears stuck in the corners of her eyes, refusing to fall. She gripped her lips with her teeth, sealing her resentment for the women who amongst themselves disapproved of Father John, but who, when confronted by their Father, remained as children—obedient to the one they served.

Sarah stood before the Nativity scene that, during the first week of January, still urged a genuflection. She did bow, and bowed again, and again, until her body fell to the ground. She realized that Jesus, hanging on the cross above the altar, was staring at her. Should she confront him? "It may be a good idea," she murmured to herself. She moved towards the cross and stared at the man with whom she was going to converse.

Their silence fell upon the church and Sarah stared at the walls as she heard her thoughts being echoed. She saw him smile. Saw him smile as her silence spoke. It was time for her to raise her objections to the man who witnessed her rape, her rage, her unwilling submission. "You are dead, aren't you?" she asked. Sarah moved towards the figure hanging on the cross. She refused to touch him, although her temptation was greater than she had anticipated. She gestured towards his lame, dead body and touched his bloody feet. The nails stuck deep into the wooden flesh and a cloth covered the genitals she motioned to see. She could not reach that high and had to fetch a ladder from the downstairs room. Standing on the ladder, Sarah could reach her right hand up and touch the statue of Jesus. The cloth around his waist was hard, like the rest of the wood, and his blue eyes warned against the atrocities she was about to commit. She stroked his one breast, but could not reach the other. Her hands covered all the areas they could reach. In an attempt to understand her forced genuflection, she giggled, then laughed so loud that the meeting room door swung open. "Get off there at once," shouted Father John. "Oh, no, what a terrible thing to do," echoed Mrs. Brown. Her voice filled the room and the emptiness of the church made it appear blasphemous. Mrs. Brown massaged her pregnant stomach and no sooner had Sarah's eyes grown still when she collapsed. Mrs. Thomas rushed to her aid and assisted Sarah with a scented handkerchief. Within seconds, Sarah knew what had happened and cried no more. She looked around the room, identified each of her onlookers and raised her body from their disgusted stares. She walked straight ahead and left the church without looking back.

Sarah knew then that her options were few. None of the women at the mothers' union could assist her. Only her own actions could save her dignity and ensure her future. As she walked briskly towards the house of her friend, she recollected her thoughts on the days she had spent at the child-care room.

She could only go to Alice and together they could work something out. Alice had encouraged Sarah to disclose her pregnancy at the mothers' meeting, and claimed that Sarah's pregnancy gave her the right to be there: she was a mother-to-be. Alice was older and lived with her mother, two sisters and her four-year-old brother. She had lost her father when she was ten years old. It was still mid-afternoon when Sarah arrived and found Alice in the company of four others. The female children were known to Sarah, and they greeted her respectfully, even though they were all the same age. They groomed each other, picking away with their afro combs and talking in soft voices about Father John and his hide-and-seek games. To Sarah's surprise, she was not Father John's treasured jewel but only his pregnant one. Each told her story while the others assisted with embraces and handkerchiefs until their voices grew louder and

fiercer. Their silence had reigned for too long. Father John had
to be dethroned from his kingdom of abuse: of rape and brutal-
ity; of destruction and robbery; of the helpings he took from
their bodies in order to do his manly job.

The female children decided upon their plan. Their combs
lay silent and patiently awaited the outcome of their courage.
Sarah left first, clenching the scribbled note that Alice obliged
her with. Each accomplice left on her own journey, in search of
the items they had all decided upon. In two hours time it would
be dark, and each would have to attend choir practice. The boys
would be with their instructor and Sarah's father would be at
home. Sarah went home to cook. She placed the note in her
panties, then removed it with the knowledge that it was not a
safe place and tied the note around her stomach. It lay crumpled
and fearless as she shivered no more.

Promptly, all the female children arrived for choir practice.
Sarah was expectedly late and presented her note to Father
John. Father John did not complain about Sarah's late arrival
since it was a usual occurrence; nor did he voice any objections
to the note requesting his urgent presence at the home of her
father. He asked that the girls sing along while he attended to
his duties and that Sarah take charge of the choir. As Father
John left, the female children all asked Sarah whether they
could leave since everybody knew that it would be some time
before Father John returned from house calls. This was, of
course, part of the plan, and Sarah granted her peers their wish
while she and Alice waited for them all to leave.

Their accomplices had already taken the shortcut to Sarah's
house where Father John would soon respond to a false house
call. At the back of the house, the female children gathered with
their cans of petroleum. Within seconds the scattered liquid surrounded the house. Sarah's father and Father John were shaking

hands and exchanging godly words of wisdom when Sarah's accomplices secured the door from the outside. Father John turned down the loud music but all was set for the final departure. As the flames ascended into the heavens and the screams of two trapped males echoed in the distance, the female children all gazed into the burning flames. Each recalled the times of their rape, their thoughts plunging into the eager fire.

When the screams of the men could no longer be heard, the female children informed the neighbours about the unfortunate event. The buckets of water, the screams and yells from church-goers who questioned the carelessness of Sarah's father with his oil lamp and cigarettes eased the pain of the younger children as they glanced at one another for support. Older men forbade the children to see the burnt bodies and several of the women cud-dled Sarah and stroked her stiff body.

Sarah looked pale in comparison and her shock was not as severe as they had anticipated.

Ayanna Black

I Write Imaginary Stories

1. seed

going it alone was never my ambition
I knew at 13 yrs old
I knew
I knew it was
not fashionable like the contents of *Vogue*
today she writes she's going it alone—
single motherhood by   choice
or despair?   the sperm bank is her obsession
and seduction
technicalizing the perfect seed for sprouting

what about the history?
smelling father's odour   smell touch and touch
like my cat Zwardi mews and mews and cuddles
up in my lap for my smell   my body contact

2. cloud

I never learned fatherly games
like my friends Carol Nerissa Pauline
when the pain was
too much for my body
to resist   I fell
in love with his absence   seven years old
and I buried him over and over
his glass casket covered
with white purple black
clouds
I write
I write imaginary
stories

3. rain

black hole
this is not your crude joke
this is a celestial reality
emptiness longings
my grandma agnes knew :
she fills me
with old photographs   him holding
me   six months old   him feeding
me   him feeding   feeding   photographs
photographs and letters and words
I cannot read words that make rain
drops I hear the sound
of raindrops I don't need raindrops
too much pain too much

grandma agnes howling sound level
with wind I'm inside
the sun his voice the healer
his face a sun
flower

4. feminism

he says feminism is not our problem
not for us it's dividing the race
I say I'm piecing
my world together already divided
before me years ago
divided
she sits regal
passionately pushing the right keys
re: feminism interspersing
her attitudes re: men
this is my centre   centre
my politics calling upon
within my healer   my survival
I write stories
I write

Claire Harris

Under Black Light

on the first saturday of every month   no
                                  matter what is/   or hoarfrost nestings
                                  scent of lilacs   rain   sky bled white
                                                              sky bruised
                                                                 shedding

on the first saturday of every month   at
                                                               eight O'clock

the girl is yOurs
the boy is yOurs

that first night my daughter shines
down to the basement
dancing for dad   the mayor
his friends   our son playing
the flute   excited
footsteps clatter   high voices proud
laughing   i say sh! break a leg!
their shimmering...

yOur friends   bottles of rye
cameras in place

                                        downstairs low
                                growls   scattered laughter
                                shouts   men clubbing
                                jubilant   below sealed doors
                                        in darkness   be
                                yOnd firelight   perimeters

no matter what
season   the girl
the bOy

                                upstairs   on the edge   i keep
                                    house   on an acreage
                                creeping towards abandoned
                            prairie   grasses waist high   yellow
                        mustard flogging bright stalks   bearded
                                    oats   the blasted rock
                                young under blue blue skies i
                        think   we are like all the best things
                                    commonplace   simple   so we
                                played there slithering up on gopher
                        holes to smash the young   unwary   hot &
                        laughing   on on to the grey broken
                                    house   hollow despite
                        empire table   chairs leaning in s/ashed
                            conversion   rosebuds straining from
                                the stalk   ghosts of windbreak
                        poplars   & there you played the fiddle
                                    threw sharp stones   till
                                                i danced

yOurs

when the house next door burnt down
we stood like a family
in the roar and bitter air
yOur hand on the girl's
shoulder   my arm around the boy
you said "finally privacy"   startled i
turned to look   yOur eyes holes
where something leapt   writhed
    boy so still
    girl rigid
i turned back to the fire   understood
i had seen flames
reflected
on the first saturday of every month   the girl
is eleven   the boy
is nine

slowly
slowly down stairs
    boy in white   & flute
    girl in pink tutu &
slippers   i remember so much
what they feared   what they dreamt:
the boy a bat carved into his hair
a red bicycle   a real easel
for the girl and one long jangling earring
hand-in-hand   they
drift   to the first landing
below tretchikoff's
cockfight   they turn
look up at
me

hOw beautiful they are   i fear the wOrld

some nights the boy gleams
for a moment   then falls into shadow
the girl is always in half
light her profile rusty   an artifact
newly unburied   their thin backs
winged   reluctant bodies foreshortened
when they look up their eyes
are caves   in the dream i lean over
banisters   in the dream i am falling towards
i am saying   go on
i am saying   you'll be all right
in the dream i am saying   make your dad
proud   i am falling through   in the dream i
wave shoo shoo   go   go on
go on in the dream   i always wake up

yOurs
you deposit them on the bed   you
put five dollars
under the pillow
yOu say   she sure can dance
i say   this is too late   troubled as
if by memory   i say they're exhausted
you say it's only the first saturday of every month
yOurs

minutes or months later
Mama   i'm tucking in a corner   Mama i
want to stop...
ballet

her face to the wall

                                        i say the kids want to stop
                            you turn   their lessons   your eyes
                 flare   air is begging my body hovers
                          over your buckle the belt circles
                  that room knuckles dance a two-step around
                          me light alive with thwacking air
              burns your brown shoes scarred like my father's
                    someone cries   cries the ceiling swings
                    open in the mirror corners scream
                          door snakes through air i am
                    on my knees head covered by my arms
                              walls sobbing   sobbing

INTERIOR: COURTROOM   DAY

Judge, lawyers, witnesses, jury, court officials.
The children sit together. On either side of them
a social worker. They are wards of the court.
There are no spectators. i am grateful.

the room	Q:	*courtswells*
muffles	You are under oath. Surely at that point you	*shimmer*
your	knew that something was terribly wrong?	*discordant*
secrets burn		*a nutcracker*
naked	A:	*seizes*
i didn't know	it was not the first time i had been beaten.	*how could i*
floors		*know*
hover the air	Q:	*the judge's*
is a dead	You expect us to believe that your hus-	*webbed wings*
zone my	band would beat you simply for saying that	*cling*

father's faces
are bear
traps faces
swing crazily
towards me
ceilings
pulse   flow
prosecutor's face
a funnel
chandeliers
ping small hail
pitching off
bins in the
barn my
mother's faces
spring at
me
i didn't know
nobody
told me
nobody you women
i am dead
centre
i am in
you women who
now live
who stare
your daughters
mark me
without care
at ease now
quake
be terrified
you women
tremble
your happy homes

your children no longer wished to take
ballet/to play the flute?

Q:
yes.

Q:
I put it to you that you enjoyed those beat-
ings. That you were a willing participant...

A:
no! no!

Q:
What happened the next day?

A:
i did what women do.

Q:
Why didn't you leave him? Take the kids...

A:
i got up to prepare supper. when he came
in, we sat down to eat...

Q:
Answer the question!

A:
where could I go that he couldn't find
me? how would we live? i phoned the
police   they said no lock could keep a
man out. would they be better off if i
were dead?

to my hair
frozen
i
lungs stuffed
accusation
drips down
window panes
walls twist
the chair
dissolves under
faces flap
over benches
tectonic
plates shift
in cracks a type
writer plays
Tchaikovsky
my mother's spin
past windows
the jury
the flute
dances past
my lips
rest on the box
without care
for the moment
i am dead
you burn
vultures
fly from your
mouths
flap
in court-air
wings
brushing
against

tremble
see clearly
your eyes
whirlpools   i
swirl   drown
your polar
eyes
the liar speaks
sweetly
the devil does
not stammer
he smiles & smiles
and listens
and speaks of love
and listens
the creak in
the heart   O
the thirst in
the heart
you women   your
grim teeth
your daughters
your babies
O

Q:
You said yourself you could not protect
them!

A:
i wanted to live... i tired
...hurt.

Q:
You have testified that you lied on the two
occasions that you went to the hospital...

A:
i was ashamed...i thought every wo...

Q:
Your pride wouldn't allow you to protect
yourself, or your children. Do you consider
yourself a fit mother?

A:
i didn't know what was happening to the
children. i didn't know...

i am a cliff
i am
granite
i live even
with your nests
on my ledges
my breasts
no
longer ache
my mouth
is a crack
i am
white cliffs
my voice:
small stones
you women
O
your daughters
will mourn
will tremble
will dissolve
your daughters
your babies
O

my eyes beg   the children
become stone

yOurs
light-years ago
you are a bolt in the sky
and you are molten brass
volcanic
you swallow the world:
look   these are hands of
a man who works hard for his family

a man   who protects
light-years ago
we shrivel   girl
is a wound   boy
ash
on the first saturday of every month
                                        at eight O'clock

in the locked
basement
      girl is yOurs
      boy is yOurs

                              brown stains on her pants
                                        she is hesitant
                                 i take her in my arms
                  this is what it means to be a woman
                     she is a woman now a woman   i
                   rock her a woman i rock and rock
                        now   woe woe woeman

i say   she is
i say she is woman now
too old to dance

relief draws its map
into your face   never
never too old to dance for Papa
he puts his arm around her
she is bone
he kisses   loudly
laughs dances her

pats her bottom   slips
her twenty dollars
it flutters to the floor

it is then i know
she is an absence
i remember

on the first saturday of every month   at eight
                        mirrors gleaming   mums in the windOw
                            house a beacon on the edge   i host
                                a card party   wives of all yOur
                    friends   later the doctor   the minister's
                                        wife   it was a test
                                how could anyOne believe

in the basement   girl
danced in her slippers
wooden zest on
her face   herself
curled tight
in her own womb   hiding
from the lascivious
gleam of their husbands   while
in the corner   nude
boy played the flute

on the first saturday of every month   you
auctioned yOur tender
flesh

                                        i am no longer

                              mama no no   nor mummy
                                    no!   and beneath
                              such wrappings there is
                                    fine dry muscle
                              i am a shelled thing
                        eaten   left is the husk   white
                                         calcareous

                                    i am all there is

on the first saturday of every month
the procedures are simple   dignified
greetings   conversation   Tchaikovsky
a wine punch in silver wedding bowls
hors d'oeuvres   we wait on Sylvie   my
throat taut   our mayor's wife always
late if she doesn't come i will knOw
if she doesn't come   the world ended
meanwhile   there are fresh blossoms
on the table   meanwhile varied linen
wild rOse china cut glass shimmering
i wait   white seethe of hope/no/hope
she comes chattering   garnished with
pearls and the night is not rags not
flaming despite   girl palely pink
and delicate curves   bOy in white &
flute   no dogs howl   air comes back
in cat's yawn   in the whispering of
cards   the even rhythm of cakes and
coffee   i am not Jael   i do not take
hammer   or nail   downstairs they
divide the spoils   to each in turn
the girl   the boy

on the first saturday of every mOnth   nO
                                                       matter the season
                                                        girl is thirteen
                                                        boy is eleven

for me there is nO
longer
a name

Uh   um   the girl stares through the open
window   in the scent of dust and hedges   um
I haven't had a period
                                           my hands clench the dough
                                           it swells through my fingers
for three months
                                                 bees in the lilacs
                                       for this moment was i born
                                  for this moment my mother's silence
                                   the handy man's fingers   her rage
                                       my father's clogging games
                                     for this moment   this girl
                                   who never mouthed a refusal

if there were rage it would stalk this page   rend/rip

she moves away   a watchful teasing
malevolence   i saw your friend
the doctor   she wants to see
you   tomorrow
it can't wait till the first saturday

                                                       i breathe in
                                   does she want to see your father

no....just my mother

she stares and stares
cabbage whites dance in the arbour

                                        i will not split
                              along seams   i wait
the door bangs shut

i laugh and laugh and lau.....

Now seventeen months later   I stand on the rim of
this new city   the woman here scribbling   bright
black in my new house its white walls white carpets
white painted sofas glass tables white lamps   she
holds out   in a black hand sprays of white gladioli
says a poem is a distraction   a wild   comfort   we
need more than poems   or hymns   she expects me to
agree   dressed all in white   I reach for the flute
fade to the window   look down on roofs riverbanks
trees dressed in a thin rime of ice   I might if
I weren't so tired but she drifts away   I begin to
play something pale   a red Honda pulls up   Adam
in denim jacket and jeans   with neon yellow sweater
waves at me   I lean against the white sill watching
Julie   her beautiful hair chopped into purple green
& pink quills   white coat open on brown sweater and
tight jeans stride the walk   a gleaming metal belt
clanging as she moves   she does not look up   I hear
a knock   pounding   shrill calls   a white seething
of breakers boils around rock   I find a smile...
I have not practised my l...

Cecil Foster

Going Home

Jerome rested on his elbows, trying to compose himself. He looked down into her face, the eyes lightly closed and fluttering. Light reflected from the outside through the window with the storm shutters and flimsy thin curtains to cast a haunting reflection on her face. The features he thought so beautiful mere minutes earlier were now almost as white as the February snow outside. He was so angry.

Only moments earlier, he had seen the same face flushed with excitement as her pleasure peaked. Only then did he allow himself to indulge in the purely physical gratification. No sooner was it over than the guilt struck. It manifested itself in debilitating anger. Starting at some point near his ass, it ripped up his spine as if someone had attached an electric wire to his balls and, at that very moment of least resistance, found the socket in the wall. The anger, the guilt were almost uncontrollable. Every fibre and nerve in his body shook and rebelled.

But the stinging jolt did something else. It petrified him, forcing him to slide off her. He sat on the edge of the bed, naked and ashamed, his head hanging as low as his pride, his lust tepidly satisfied but his heart hollow. His spirits were defeated and deflated like an empty balloon. Every statement of the conversation he had overheard earlier in the night came flooding back. Every word pounded in his head like a reggae bass drum, taunting him. Nothing he could do silenced the voices. They had moved into his head and taken over. He could no longer ignore their accusations of betrayal.

In this daze, Jerome heard a loud sucking of teeth, the way West Indians show disgust. To his horror, he realized he was making the sound. Of all the responses possible to assuage this bolt of anger dashing through his body, all he could offer was a sickening sucking of the teeth—an act that would be deemed the epitome of bad manners in polite society. A society like the restricted community into which he was now so openly welcomed; the one that only a few hours earlier had fêted him as one of them: a natural achiever who had so much to give; who, despite his skin colour, so easily met its rigid qualifications for adoption.

This society had rewarded him well. Earlier in the evening, it had not only marked his acceptance and arrival with the social event of the year, but had not frowned when he chose for his trophy the most eligible female executive from among them, a woman who had gone out of her way to be seen standing at his side all night.

Jerome stared through the window. Somewhere in the distance was the pinnacle of one of Toronto's tall buildings. On top of it, partly hidden by the low flying clouds, was a red light, warning of poor weather. It was shining through the winter storm outside. Jerome had reached his pinnacle, something he had worked and suffered so long to achieve, but there was nothing to signal how he really felt. There was no red light to indicate the furious storms raging inside him.

Who was he angry with and why? Jerome tried to reason. Himself, or the white body nestling in the bed? He glanced at the woman, who was resting in the serenity of satisfaction. Contentment enveloped her, like the sheets she was pulling over her shoulders. Such restfulness could only be the testament of inner fulfilment, of her happiness and approval of his performance. Jerome wondered if it occurred to her that he might be tormented, fighting a conscience that chose to be too active on this very night. A conscience that kept taunting him for being used, like a piece of meat, for reducing himself to nothing more than a symbol.

Maybe he shouldn't care so much what other people were saying. He had paid his dues. He was entitled to the fruits of his success. Nobody was going to live his life or put restrictions on him. Nobody had any right to tell him with whom he should choose to share his well-earned achievements. Nor did anyone have any right to look on him as a symbol of their success, to claim his ascension as their achievement, to demand that he share his personal accomplishments communally. Nobody had the right to anoint him as a social role model, to demand that he be responsible for the success of any particular race. He would not bow to any peer pressure. He would choose for himself, socialize with whomever he wanted.

But this reasoning did not wash. He still could not explain his torment. If he enjoyed his personal success so much, why was he so angry at this moment of absolute and supreme triumph—a moment that ordinarily should be so soft and reassuring? He should have quietly fallen asleep, sweet success and acceptance rocking him in their arms.

Instead, he was furious. He had heard other men who had gone with whores swear how, at such critical moments, they too had to fight to control the urge to strike out, to repel, reject.

How they felt unclean, like someone sacrificing everything to get a cherished victory only to discover, at the very moment of receipt, that what was purchased was phony and vacuous—a mere Pyrrhic victory destroying the soul. He never thought it would happen to him. The men who told him such stories were unsophisticated. They were not like him. They had not climbed to the pinnacle and looked back down on the people they had risen from among. They did not know that the mere act of reaching such lofty heights numbed the sensibilities that caused such regrets. Now that he was facing his own crisis, the violent emotions were unexplainable. He was no longer the type of man who had to deal with such misgivings! Yet all he knew was how angry and defiled he felt, as if he had auctioned his very soul.

"What's the matter, dear?" she whispered, turning on her side, displaying the smooth hump of her hips under the sheet. She ran her hand casually along his thigh and across his broad back. The touches seemed no different from earlier. Yet they made him feel as if, by touching him this way, she was laying claim to him, as if she really possessed him. As if she wanted to talk to him, to be caressed or even to be with him for the rest of the night as promised. He chose not to answer. She continued to massage his back. Anger consumed him.

"Upset?" she persisted. Her voice was low and stealthy. The other voices conspired to drown it out, the way the immune system leaps into action at the first sign of a virus. His conscience struggled to decipher what the voices were saying, to ask them why they were spitefully tormenting him. "Is something wrong?"

"Um." Jerome did not know if he was answering Joanne on the bed or the nagging voices beating his conscience into submission.

He got off the bed, steadying himself as the water swished around in the leather mattress. He picked up his pants and underwear from the floor beside the chair. In the shadowy light, he was reminded of all the trappings and trimmings of the good life that the woman on the bed offered: the easy credit, the name recognition, the absence of worry over how the expenses for the lifestyle he so badly craved could be met. A divorce could be arranged so easily. Then everything he wanted, had worked for, would be waiting for him in this very room, with all its enticing perfumes.

This was an address to enhance his curriculum vitae, the ideal one to go with the new title and address on his business cards. Around him was luxury: the Jacuzzi mere steps away, the well-stocked bar waiting to serve guests, the elaborate home-entertainment system, the condo without one cent's mortgage outstanding. They were all his for the taking. One of the perks for having finally achieved his proper status in life. This was the kind of place to which he could willingly invite important friends and associates without being ashamed or apologetic. He wouldn't have to explain that the living room was too small, the basement too rough for people who lived in Rosedale or along Bayview. And Joanne would be the ideal person to stand by his side, to chit-chat knowledgeably with the important guests and to help him say and do the right thing. Then, the next day, he would stand by her side as she did the entertaining. They would be such a team. She would be the perfect social coach. She was willing to teach him, to sandpaper his edges.

He should be rationally, unemotionally comparing these things against what he had at home. The small house with the big mortgage. The fact that he must be the one to pull his partner up the economic and social ladder. He had to do it by himself, not knowing when he made a mistake, unsure of his social graces. His wife was even more ignorant than he of this new culture into which he was being immersed, into which he was seeping. She could not tell him if he was doing right; she was even too frightened to encourage him to entertain his clients and colleagues at home. A few minutes into a conversation she would start doubting herself, glancing at him with pleading eyes to rescue her. She had not kept pace with him.

She might have been the right woman when he was starting out, struggling. As a nurse, she enjoyed a secure salary by the standards she had set herself. And she knew how to get him to relax. She knew which pills soothed his throbbing headaches after a long day at the office. Her trained fingers readily found the deep knots in his shoulders and back and released them so skilfully. But beyond that she was not much help, certainly not in the areas he needed assistance, where Joanne stood head and shoulders above her.

They had outgrown each other, the same way he had outpaced the men who had complained of feeling so hollow after tasting the forbidden fruit. It should be more than tempting for him to want to stay in this cosy bedroom so high above the city. He should be counting his blessings, trying desperately (or at least a bit harder) to extinguish the anger. At least he should be willing to pretend, to hide his disgust. He should settle back and enjoy, knowing that daylight would bring him to his senses when he faced the outside world.

Silently, he slipped one leg into the underpants, suddenly becoming aware of the excruciating stillness in the room, of Joanne's breathing, of the cars struggling to negotiate the treacherous snowbound roads outside, of the snowploughs passing with feverish noises. The storm was still raging. Chances were some of the very men cleaning the streets down below were once his closest friends, his people. He could almost hear them laughing and swearing at the weather, even though in their hearts they were glad the heavens had opened up because the storm provided them with jobs, work the elite of the city never considered for themselves. In his mind, he could hear them loud and clear, even from this perch on the thirtieth floor in the heart of the business district. Earlier in the night, the lobby security was ready to throw him out until Joanne appeared and took his arm. Now, from this foreign land, he could hear the noises below. He wanted to be anywhere except in this bedroom.

Joanne must have sensed his mood. She was saying nothing, just watching him, resignedly not moving. He could feel her eyes boring into him with the kind of sixth sense a bird relies on to detect an approaching cat.

"I'm going home," he said laconically.

"What about the snow and the rain?" she whispered, sounding sleepy. Perhaps she was not really concerned. Just going through the motions. Having sensed his aloofness, maybe she was just pretending to care. "It's too slippery to drive and you've been drinking."

"I'll be okay."

"Take a cab. Get the car in the morning."

"No, I'll be okay." He glanced out the window at the eerie skyline. The way she spoke in commands irritated him. Millions of tiny snowflakes were fluttering through the light, forming a white blanket on the roofs of the houses in the distance. Somewhere down there in the snow, his brand-new, company-provided BMW was parked. It would take him a good twenty minutes to clean the three hours of snow off the car and clear a path through the pile of ice deposited by the ploughs at the entrance. And yes, he shouldn't be driving. But somewhere else in the city peace and quiet were irresistibly beckoning. Jerome knew he had to get out. There was no way he could keep his promise to stay with this woman for the entire night and possibly beyond.

He glanced again at the light on top of the building in the distance. It was still red, but with more of a pinkish hue. He did not know if his eyes were playing tricks. Maybe they were tired from such a long day. Or maybe the light was in fact changing. He was weary. He had to go to his bed.

A few hours earlier, if anyone had told him, even as a joke, that he would be turning his back on the woman in the bed Jerome would not have believed it. Nobody worked and schemed to achieve a coveted prize simply to walk away from it. Dreams were to be treasured, the sweet taste of such achievements savoured. Anyone who knew Jerome Downes knew he was not one to miss opportunities. He would do whatever was necessary to succeed.

But something had happened during the night.

He left home dressed in a rented tuxedo in time to make an entrance on the banquet floor of the swanky Four Seasons Hotel, purposely alone and looking dapper. Only two things were on his mind: having a good time while being officially inducted as a member of what his friends in business school called the "captains of industry" club; and at the end of the night leaving with the sexy Joanne Delores, chief operating officer for Comex Industries, and touted as the company's next president and chief executive.

Joanne had called earlier in the day, supposedly to ask if it was still all right for her to turn up at his party without an escort. As if she really expected him to believe a woman headed for the chief executive suite of a multibillion-dollar company would have trouble finding a male companion for the night. Jerome took this question for what it was—and told her he too would be single for the night.

"Do you have any plans for after the reception?" he asked.

"Not really."

"Maybe we can spend the night getting to know each other a little better," he offered.

"All night?"

"If you want."

"Is that a promise, Mr. Downes?" she teased.

"You betcha," he said into the phone. She laughed and hung up.

When he got off the elevator, Joanne was waiting for him. She was impeccably dressed in one of the most exquisite and revealing dresses he had ever seen. She came straight towards him. Instead of the standard firm business handshake, she planted such wet kisses on his cheeks that she had to use his handkerchief to remove the red lipstick. Her action was a clear signal to everyone: Jerome Downes had arrived in more than one way.

She stayed at his side while he made the rounds and the introductions, signalling to all other women to stay clear of her possession. This was a woman who, according to rumours, was so busy climbing the corporate ladder that she could not find time for matters of the heart. She had turned down more than one well-heeled suitor, if the rumours were correct. She had told the business magazines she didn't find men in business attractive. If she had time to choose a date, it would be someone in sports, not the businessmen she dealt with every day. Yet, she chose to be with him. What more could he want? Jerome asked himself.

But usually, it's the small things that matter. He was standing by the table with the gift, getting ready for the speeches. They were talking, perhaps not knowing he overheard them. Every word from the two black women, the only other black faces in the room, was enough to cut his heart out. He was glad he did not meet them. From what they were saying, he could not look these women in the face and not feel guilty. For the rest of the evening, their voices haunted him.

"I guess there is no hope for our people," the tall slim woman was saying. "I really wonder why I would bother to come to a celebration like this."

"Me too," the other woman said. "Isn't it strange? I tell yuh: strange things happen in this world. A man being fêted for his achievement as a black man trying his hardest not to appear to be black."

"That happens all the time, doesn't it?" the first woman said. "Take the fellow that is the U.S. Supreme Court judge. The same thing. I guess I'll never understand why, as soon as one of the brothers reaches any level of success, he always has to look for a white woman to make him feel accomplished. They simply become a toy, a possession of these women. What's wrong with our sisters that the brothers treat them so? As soon as they become successful they become a traitor to their people."

Jerome kept his head straight. His wineglass was empty, his lips were now parched. He was tempted to refill his glass before the presentations started. But the conversation had caught his ear, particularly the word *traitor*. He had never heard anyone talk about him in such a manner. He had grown accustomed to the praise, so bountiful of late, as if he was now faultless. Something more than the obvious criticism grabbed his attention, struck a chord deep inside him. He wanted to hear more.

"What a fine hunk, too," the other said. "What a pity he couldn't find a sister to help uplift. But he'll soon learn his lesson. As soon as he stumbles or screws up, the very people he's so wrapped up in, they will be the ones to knife him in the back. Mark my words, he'll have to come back home to his own people, just like any old Joe. He'll soon find out how lonely it is at the top; to be the only black face, too. His biggest mistake will be to trust these people. Any sister with his interest at heart can tell him that. But you know how blind the black men are sometimes."

"It's not only a question of uplifting just any sister," the first woman was saying. "I'm sure at one point or another there must have been a sister in his life who helped him to get where he is when he was nothing. But now the brother's riding high. He has to accept all the trappings that society tells him a black man needs to look successful—the white picket fence, the blond wife, the two-and-a-half curly-haired kids and a white dog. I tell yuh, I don't think there is much hope for us as a people."

Suddenly, Jerome doubted himself. Was he hearing correctly? Maybe the alcohol was numbing his senses, making him hear things that were only inside his head. Nobody used those clichés any more. Such language was a relic from another era, thirty years ago or even longer. Could it be that his conscience, loosened by the vintage French wine and the anxiety of the evening, was dredging up bits from all the speeches he had heard and the books he had read when he was in the vanguard of the now-dead black-consciousness movement?

Of course, he was still a pioneer. The newspapers and magazines acknowledged that he was the highest-ranking black business executive in the country, and his company chairman had stressed that his promotion had nothing to do with his colour. Still, appointments to the executive suites were such a rarity for people like him that this one had to be celebrated as another black breaking through. In fact, his appointment was a coup for someone with no established roots in Canadian business and no long family ties. Even if his company pretended otherwise, his promotion had to be celebrated for its symbolism. Maybe his confused mind was merely putting one night's celebration in the context of a historical struggle.

"That's the way this society toys with us," the second woman said. "It preys on our insecurities; makes us feel we have to measure success according to their benchmarks. Destroys everything we built up over the years. For me, the sorrowful thing is the brothers. They are so psychologically beaten down, they're the ones most vulnerable. No matter how strong and boastful they appear, no matter how smart, they're always the weaker ones, the exposed and vulnerable flank."

Joanne brought over the glass of wine. She took her position at his side. Jerome thought he heard one of the women suck her teeth, or perhaps both of them did it at the same time.

The conversation was a time-release capsule placed in his mind. Gradually, it sapped his enthusiasm over the night as the implications continued to haunt him. By the time he and Joanne left the reception, it was snowing heavily. But they still decided to go through with plans for a quiet dinner, her treat to him. She ordered the champagne and they drank, indulged and flirted. From very early, it was quite clear he was totally in control. Nothing could go wrong. She was like putty in his hands, so malleable. Yet he felt she was the one shaping him into something hideous, a distorted figure he might not want to see the next time he passed by a mirror.

By the time they left the restaurant, the snow had piled up. Cars were skidding on the roads. The earlier conversation was racking his brain, vying so much for attention at times that he didn't hear what Joanne was saying. Outside the restaurant, she wrapped the fur coat around her and held on to his arm, once again as if she possessed him. Once again, in his mind, Jerome heard the women sucking their teeth. He drove to her condominium. He parked the car in front of the building, even though she had suggested he use the underground parking since he was staying all night.

"The car will be warm and dry," she said. "We can have breakfast at my club. You'd be surprised at the amount of business I complete over croissants and coffee. But it's crowded and you have to get there on time. Park the car underground."

"No, I'll leave it here." This should have been the first sign to both of them he might not be spending the entire night away from home. Neither of them took the hint.

Jerome had never thought of himself as weak or a traitor. But now, as he sat in the BMW, encapsulated in the fresh leather smell of the interior, he could still hear the women in his mind. What they had said did not apply to him. He knew that for sure; he could pick apart the logic in their arguments if he cared enough to think at all about the foolishness they had said. Anyone who ever met him knew absolutely he wasn't one to be trapped that easily; he was independent in mind and spirit; nobody could force him to accept their standards. Nobody who knew him would dare say he was betraying some racial pride. If he changed, adopted new friends and lifestyles, it was because he wanted to, because he saw the way to a better life. Because he didn't want to feel he was the property of anybody, not even of the people he came from, the same people whose sons and daughters were writing him almost daily asking for jobs and for advice on what university courses they should take if they wanted to be as great a success as he.

At the same time, he could acknowledge the small bit of truth in the women's conversation, but only if they were talking about men generally and not about him specifically. He knew how difficult and frustrating it was coming from the other side and pretending to be part of the business class, knowing most of the executives genuinely believed he didn't belong among them.

There was a time when every morning, on leaving home, he felt he was putting on a mask, or, he reflected on his way up the elevator, that he had to step across a gulf to get to his desk. For the next ten or twelve hours, he pretended to be who and what he wasn't. He pretended to share, understand and care about conversations about spending weekends at cottages in the country as his colleagues did, all the time knowing his activities had been restricted to the city life he could hardly afford. Or he pretended he had thousands of dollars to invest in registered retirement plans, that he too had the monstrous problem of trying to find the right accountant or tax planner. He too would talk glibly about buying stocks at discount for his personal portfolio, discuss favourable commission rates he was paying stockbrokers, knowing full well he could not afford one. Then, at the end of the day, he took off the mask, stepped back over the gulf and became himself again.

But because he had come from people struggling like himself to get ahead, no law said he had to remain among them. He had worked hard and mastered the other man's lifestyle. When he went to business luncheons and receptions, he could now mix freely, not feeling out of place and resented. He had successfully negotiated the crossover as well as could be expected. This final elevation was his chance to submerge himself totally in this culture so that the mask would become his permanent features.

Driving conditions were worse than he thought. The road was reduced to one lane and the defrosters were working overtime to clear the windshield. Jerome wanted so much more in life—things he could not get, no matter how high he rose as a business executive, if he did not change his lifestyle, if he did not start associating with people from whom he could learn. The self-doubts had returned. In his head he could hear Joanne talking softly, whispering they should talk again soon. He would definitely have to set up a new home if he really wanted to get ahead. If not with Joanne, certainly with someone else, but preferably with a business woman. In the morning, he'd call Joanne first thing. Croissants and coffee sounded great.

Jerome felt the warmth of familiarity as soon as he walked in the door. The heavy load on his shoulders lifted instantly. He was on familiar turf; in the darkness and without searching, he knew where to find every cup, fork and spoon; where every chair and table was, the VCR and television, and the framed pictures and university parchments.

Not bothering to take off his coat, he tiptoed upstairs and peeked into the room where the kids were sleeping, blissfully unaware of their father's plans and his interrupted night. Going to each bed, he pulled the blankets over the kids and kissed each of them. He knew he was going to miss them so much if he went through with his plans for another home. So often he had tried to form the right words in his mind; to have the speech prepared, so it would be easy to explain why he had to leave for his fulfilment, to achieve his dreams, to go after his destiny. He hoped they would understand. Closing the door quietly behind him, he tried to dismiss those thoughts from his mind. He tried to smother the disapproving lecture from earlier in the night.

From the hallway, he could hear the quiet snoring coming from his bedroom. She was asleep, perhaps unaware of the night and the big reception. He hadn't told her. Yet it was hard to think a woman who had spent so many years with him didn't know what was going on. Purposely, he had chosen not to tell her. He didn't want her at the reception to cramp his style. In any case, he had told himself, she wouldn't want to be there anyway. She always complained she didn't like hanging out with boring business people, as she called them. She didn't have to put up with them as she didn't have to cross that gulf every day to make a living. "I like being myself," he heard her say in his head. "I'll always be me. I can't be anybody else. I hope people will accept me as I am or to hell with them."

So he hadn't told her and she knew not to wait up for him as he was late most nights. That was why it made so much sense to latch on to a woman like Joanne, who was so much like him, who enjoyed the same people and business events and who, at his side, was such a beautiful enhancement, like the final piece of a jigsaw puzzle.

No matter what those women at the party thought, his choice, although painful, was nonetheless inevitable. In a few hours, he would be at the club in time for one of those power breakfasts. He might never return to this home. Maybe his lawyer would make the arrangements. He'd ask her to make an appointment for him to see the kids so he could explain his actions to them face to face.

Jerome pushed the door open and slipped in, hoping to undress in the warm light reflecting through the window from the snow piled high in the backyard. She must have heard him or maybe, after all these years, even in sleep her senses were so attuned to him that she was instantly aware of his presence.

"You're home," she muttered, turning on her side to make room for him in the bed.

"Yes. I'm home. Tonight I..."

But he didn't finish. She was already snoring peacefully. He looked at her, clothed in the warmth of the room, her hair in long, controllable braids. The clock on the bureau ticked softly. The anger in him dissipated. Jerome looked at his own perfectly shaped shadow across the bed, cutting his wife at the waist. The mask had slipped again. He wondered what colour the light on top of the building was, the light he could no longer see from this part of the city. The voices in his head reminded him the shadow on the bed was also naked and vulnerable.

Makeda Silvera

Her Head a Village

Her head was a noisy village, one filled with people, active and full of life, with many concerns and opinions. Children, including her own, ran about. Cousins twice removed bickered. A distant aunt, Maddie, decked out in two printed cotton dresses, a patched-up pair of pants and an old fuzzy sweater, marched up and down the right side of her forehead. Soon she would have a migraine. On the other side, a pack of idlers lounged around a heated domino game, slapping the pieces hard against her left forehead. Close to her neck sat the gossiping crew, passing around bad news and samples of malicious and scandalous tales. The top of her head was quiet. Come evening this would change, with the arrival of schoolchildren; when the workers left their factories and offices, the pots, banging dishes and televisions blaring would add to the noisy village.

The black woman writer had been trying all month to write an essay for presentation at an international forum for Third World women. She was to address the topic, "Writing As a Dangerous Profession." This was proving to be more difficult as the weeks passed. She pleaded for quiet, but could silence only the children.

The villagers did not like her style of writing, her focus and the new name she called herself—feminist. They did not like her choice of lovers, her spending too many hours behind her desk or propped up in her bed with paper and pen or book. The workers complained that she should be in the factories and offices with them; the idlers said she didn't spend much time playing with them and the gossiping crew told so many tales that the woman writer had trouble keeping her essay separate from their stories. Some of the villagers kept quiet, going about their business, but they were too few to shut out the noise. Maddie did not often side with the writer, but neither did she poke at her. She listened and sometimes smiled at the various expressions that surfaced on the woman writer's face. Maddie stood six feet tall with a long, stern face and eyes like well-used marbles. The villagers said Maddie was a woman of the spirits, a mystic woman who carried a sharpened pencil behind her ear. She walked about the village all day, sometimes marching loudly, and other times quietly. Some days she was seen talking to herself.

"When I first come to this country, I used to wear one dress at a time. But times too hard, now you don't know if you coming or going, so I wear all my clothes. You can't be too sure of anything but yourself. So I sure of me, and I wear all my clothes on my back. And I talk to meself, for you have to know yourself in this time."

The villagers didn't know what to make of her. Some feared her, others respected her. The gossipers jeered behind her back.

Plugging her ears against spirit-woman Maddie, the black woman writer sat in different places she thought would be good to her. She first sat behind her desk, but no words came. It was not so much that there were no words to write down—there were many—but the villagers were talking all at once and in so many tongues that it was hard for her to hold onto their words. Each group wanted her to feature them in the essay.

Early in the morning, after her own children left for school, she tried to write in her bed. It was a large queen-size pine bed with five pillows in a small room on the second floor. The room was a pale green and the ceilings a darker shade of green—her favourite colour. She was comfortable there and had produced many essays and poems from that bed. Its double mattress almost reached the ceiling. She felt at peace under the patchwork blanket. It took her back to her grandparents' wooden house a mile from the sea in another village, the tropical one where she was born. Easter lilies, powder-puff trees, dandelions and other wild flowers circled the house. She saw a red-billed Streamertail, the a yellow-crowned night heron and a white-bellied Caribbean dove, their familiar voices filling her head. "*Quaart, Tlee-oo-ee, cruuuuuuuuu,*" and other short repeated calls.

She wrote only lists of "To do's":
washing
cleaning
cooking
laundry
telephone calls
appointments.
At the edge of the paper birds took flight.

Nothing to do with writing, she thought. On days like these, convinced that she would get no writing done, she left the village and lunched with friends. She did not tell her friends about the village in her head. They would think her crazy, like Maddie. When she was alone, after lunch, scores of questions flooded her head.

What conditions are necessary for one to write?
What role do children play in a writer's creativity?
Is seclusion a necessary ingredient?
Questions she had no answers for.

Sometimes she holed up in the garden shed at the edge of the backyward. She had cleared out a space and brought in a kerosene heater. The shed faced south. Old dirty windows ran the length of it and the ceiling's cracked blue paint threatened to fall. There she worked on an oversize ill-kept antique desk, a gift from a former lover. She had furnished the space with two chairs, a wooden crate stacked with a dictionary and a few books, a big armchair dragged from the neighbour's garbage, postcards pasted on the walls to remind her of Africa. There were a few things from her village: coconut husks, ackee seeds, photographs of birds, flowers and her grandparents' house near the sea.

One afternoon, however, the villagers discovered the shed and moved in. The idlers set up their gambling table. Gossip-mongers sat in a large area and Maddie walked around quietly and read everything written on every piece of paper. Soon they all wanted to read her essay. The idlers made fun of her words. The gossip-mongers said they had known all along what she would write. Offices and factories closed early, as the others hurried into the shed to hear what all the shouting was about.

They were all talking at once, with varying opinions.

"Writing is not a dangerous profession, writing is a luxury!" shouted one of the workers.

"Many of us would like to write but can't. We have to work, find food to support our families. Put that in your essay."

"What's this?" another villager asked, pulling at the paper.

"Look here, read here, something about woman as a lover and the danger of writing about that."

The black woman writer's head tore in half as the villagers snatched at the paper. She shouted as loud as she could that there was more to the paper than that.

"See for yourselves—here, read it, I am also writing about the economics of writing, problems of women writers who have families." Almost out of breath, she continued, "See, I also wrote about cultural biases."

"Cultural biases," snarled a cold, grating voice. "Why not just plain old racism? What's wrong with that word?" Before she could answer, another villager who was jumping up and down silenced the rest of them. "This woman thing can't go into paper. It wouldn't look right to talk about that at a Third World Conference." They all shouted in agreement.

She felt dizzy. Her ears ached. Her mouth and tongue were heavy. But she would not give in. She tried to block them out by calling up faces of the women she had loved. But she saw only the faces of the villagers and heard only the sounds of their loud chatter.

"No one will write about women lovers. These are not national concerns in Third World countries. These issues are not relevant. These," they shouted, "are white bourgeois concerns!"

Exhausted, the black woman writer tried again. "All I want to do is to write something about being a black lesbian in a North American city. One where white racism is cloaked in liberalism and where black homophobia..." They were not listening. They bombarded her with more questions.

"What about the danger of your writing being the definitve word for all black women? What about the danger of writing in a liberal white bourgeois society and of selling out? Why don't you write about these things?"

She screamed at them to shut up and give her a voice, but they ignored her and talked even louder.

"Make it clear that you, as a black woman writer, are privileged to be speaking on a panel like this."

"And what about the danger of singular achievement?" asked a worker.

"Woman lover," sniggered another. "What about the danger of writing about racism—police harrassment—murders of our villagers?"

Many times during the month the black woman writer would scream at them to shut up. And when she succeeded in muting their voices she was tired because they refused to speak one at a time.

On days like these the black woman writer escaped from the garden shed to play songs by her favourite blues singer, drink bottles of warm beer and curl up in her queen-size pine bed. she held on to the faces of her lovers and tried to forget the great difficulty in writing the essay.

The writer spent many days and nights staring at the blank white paper in front of her. The villagers did not ease up. They criticized the blank white paper. It was only a few days before the conference. "You have to start writing," they pressured her. "Who is going to represent us?"

Words swarmed around her head like wasps. There was so much she wanted to say about "Writing As a Dangerous Profession," about dangers to *her* as a black woman, writer, lesbian. At times, she felt that writing the paper was hopeless. Once she broke down and cried in front of the villagers. On this particular day, as the hour grew close, she felt desperate—suicidal, in fact. The villagers had no sympathy for her.

"Suicide? You madder than Maddie!" they jeered. "Give Maddie the paper and let her use her pencil," they heckled.

"I'm not mad," she protested with anger. "Get out of my

head. Here"—she threw the blank paper on the ground—"write, write, you all write."

"But you are the writer," they pestered her. They were becoming hostile and vicious. The woman writer felt as if her head would burst.

She thought of Virginia Woolf's *A Room of One's Own*. She wondered if Woolf had had a village in her head.

She took to spending more time in bed with a crate of warm beer at the side. Her eyes were red from worry, not enough sleep and too much drink. She studied her face in a small hand-mirror, examining the lines on her forehead. They were deep and pronounced, lines she had not earned, even with the raising of children, writing several essays and poetry books, cleaning, cooking and caring for lovers. She gazed at all the books around her and became even more depressed.

Interrupted by the angry voices of the villagers, overwhelmed by the force of their voices, she surrendered her thoughts to them.

"Well, what are you going to write? We have ideas to give you." The black woman writer knew their ideas. They were not new, but she listened.

"Write about women in houses without electricity."

"Write about the dangers of living in a police state."

"Write about Third World issues."

"Write about...about..."

"Stick to the real issues that face black women writers."

"Your sexuality is your personal business."

"We don't want to hear about it, and the forum don't want to know."

They accused her of enjoying the luxury of being a lesbian in a decaying society, of forgetting about their problems.

She tried to negotiate with them. "Listen, all I want is a

clear head. I promise to write about your concerns." But they disagreed. "We gave you more than enough time, and you've produced nothing." They insisted that they all write the paper. She was disturbed by their criticism. She would never complete the paper with so many demands. The black woman writer was full of despair; she wanted to explain to the villagers, once again, that what makes writing dangerous for her was who she was— black/woman/lesbian/mother/worker... But they would not let her continue. In angry, harsh voices they pounded her head. "You want to talk about sexuality as a political issue? Villagers are murdered every time they go out, our young people jailed and thrown out of schools." Without success, she explained that she wanted to talk about all the dangers of writing. "Have you ever heard of, read about lesbians in the Third World? They don't have the luxury of sitting down at an international forum and discussing this issue so why should you?"

Her head blazed; her tiny tight braids were like coals on fire. The villagers stayed in her head, shouting and laughing. She tried closing her eyes and massaging her forehead. With her eyes still closed, she eased her body onto the couch. Familiar footsteps sounded at the side of her head. Maddie appeared. "All this shouting and hollering won't solve anything—it will only make us tired and enemies. We all have to live together in this village." Not one villager joked about her two dresses, pants and sweater. Not one villager had anything to say about the pencil stuck in her hair, a pencil she never used. Maddie spoke for a long time, putting the villagers to sleep.

The black woman writer slept late, dreaming first of her grandparents' village and then of her lovers. Now Maddie's face came. She took Maddie's hand and they set out down the village streets, through the fields of wild flowers, dandelion and Easter lilies. Maddie took the pencil from her head and began to write. With Maddie beside her, she awoke in a bed of wild flowers, refreshed.

Frederick Ward

Kitten Face

I'M WAITING to be punished. Mama says she's "HAD ENOUGH!" She's been "TRYING TO TEACH" me "SOMETHING"——I thought I'd learned it. Anyway, I'm waiting here in Mama's computer room, hoping when Papa comes home he find me at the computer and think I'm learning something. But I'm also waiting to be punished...waiting for Papa to come home so she can tell him——and he'll punish me, all right.

I tried to figure out how he'd do it, and I been practising. I stood in the corner for a few minutes. I spanked my hand with the other——he might do one of those. I spoke scary to myself, all the things he'd say to my sister when he's mad at her and all the things he's say to me when he's mad——some of them, the things I heard him say when he'd talk back to Mama, and I say some things the way Gramma Shu says them, *ghost-like*. I say them under my top lip, wrinkled my eyebrows and dipped them from the middle of my bow'd head into my chin so I could "*pour forth*" the "*madness in my mind*" down through my nose, same as Papa do: "YOUUUuuuuuuu..."——say it all to myself, just to see if I could scare myself into "*preparedness.*"

"YOUR PAPA GONNA GET YOU TWICE FOR YOUR DAY...AND GET YOUR EYEBROWS OFF THE TOP OF YOUR HEAD, YOU AIN'T THAT INNO-CENT."

Mama's voice were little through her teeth, echoed in me from this morning——have her finger focused right tween my eyes, she says:

"YOU THINK YOU'RE SMART, DON'T YOU? WHAT THE HELL YOU THINK YOU WERE TRYING TO DO, MISTER EDISON?"

I'm in trouble twice cause I discovered I could unscrew the wall socket. I discovered, when I put my finger into the wall socket, it made me jump and feel funny all at the same time. It hurt my finger a bit but the hurt went away when I sucked at it. Then I'd try the new discovery again——all in the last week I done it. This week Mama caught me...she ran me around the house shouting:

"CAUGHT YOU/CAUGHT YOU!"

I'm in trouble again cause I tried to shorten my prayer to God. You see, Mama grabbed me up from the floor when she "caught" me. It scared me, and we both went to screaming. She run through every room in the house, hugging me till it hurt, and her shouting:

"My to mercy, not my baby/my baby my baby child! O Lord! Please...O hold Your wrath gainst me and my guilt. That stranger *talked* his way into my bedroom. Not my baby, my baby boy. No, no, no."

Everything vibrated in her neck and head, chattering her teeth. She grabbed my head and pressed it gainst hers and her vibrations come'd onto me, the same nearly as the buzzing I got when I put my finger into the light socket——but not the hurt. Mama bent quick, sucking in air, come'd up at the silence—— maybe The Lord, weren't that mad at her——and swallowed it.

Mama let me down-slide to the floor. I smeared tears and snot on her tween her breasts. She pressed a hand there and drawed it up on her fingers:

"You got a snout full of slop, boy. Go blow your nose. Wash your face." She say this calm as what nothing never happened——say it with her fingers making slow circlings in the tears-n-snot, then wiped them dry in the palm of her other hand——staring. Gramma Shu spoke ghostly once of Mama's staring, say Mama:

"...at the blue and golds chilowi widgeons mongst wild parsley wallpaper... Staring, plaintively."

Mama closed her eyes and looked at me——I could tell it were me cause her eyes rolled up under her eyelids in my direction——She said:

"Get on in there at that table, after, and eat something—— and say your blessing before God, afore you eat. Hear?"

Her

"Answer me boy!"

bumped into my

"Yessum."

I washed! I were hungry and "Too anxious you were" to eat fast. I got over the breakfast bowl and says,

"O God, O God, this is a recording, this is a recording, this is a recording..."

Mama broke my prayer with,

"YOU MOST BOUND TO MAKE TROUBLE FOR YOURSELF THIS DAY, AIN'T YOU? AIN'T YOU, BOY!?... WHEN YOUR PAPA GETS/I SWEAR..."

(I ain't say nothing.)

She shout,

"HUSH YOUR BACKTALK TO ME BOY! You f-o-o-l."

She stepped my way but thought on it——had enough. Mama say she had had enough of me.

She sent me to my room but I sneaked in here to the computer. The computer talks to me and I tell it things. You see, when my mama doesn't want me to know what she and the neighbour-woman are talking about, they spell it out. Mama alerts her, says, "Important," and she spells the rest out. I can't read yet, but I can, and do, collect the letters to my memory and I run here to the computer and tell it. Some times the computer knows.

"Computer, what is *f-o-o-l*——huh?"

COMPUTER: F-O-O-L: British cookery. A dish made of fruit, scalded or stewed, crushed and mixed with cream or the like...

"Mama didn't say it that way, computer."

It's a good thing Sister's acting funny these days cause I'd be in real trouble tonight. I reasoned that Sister and the dog were eating together cause she never eat nothing at the table and her stomach were swelling——more often she never come'd to the table to eat with the family. I took to following her about but I were afraid. The safe thing to do were just be around her shadow. Whenever her shadow be around I'd go sit next to it, walk with it——I kept my distance with her ceptin for my eyes and ears. I put her shadow in one, its echo in the other. It's fun watching her shadow talk——caused a staring to occupy itself in me. I even crawled inside of Sister's shadow once——after Sister were crying——a *"lonesome spot"* come'd in on Sister's shadow, took its place in droops and sags. I were sitting next of it——when Sister's shadow say to its stomach,

I am so ugly
I can't tell if I am sick
The only tears I can manage for myself
Come when I think of you

I moved with the shadow outside onto the porch where it sit on the steps. Sister planted her elbows on her knees, "*rest her* life"...rest her forehead on the back edge of her palms stretched——cupped towards "The WHERES." Her head were covered and bent over her right shoulder——

"...*forgetful under the weight of a large towel...*"
Gramma Shu say:
"*The crown Shaw of a boxer after losing.*"

I imagined Sister's eyes, if opened, black holes with the worrisome buzz-passing, in and out of, then landing of a greenfly, its hind legs scratching its wings, itching up a few blinks in Sister's stare neath the towel.
"*Such an eyeless face lie next of her,*
torn out of a round loaf of brown bread
dropped in the dirt by the steps."

I were most attracted to Sister's feet: swollen, wrinkled and mud chooked. Mama, later, telling my image of Sister to the neighbour woman, say,
"Sister having (Important): M-O-R-N-I-N-G S-I-C-K-N-E-S-S."
Mama say I musn't struggle with Sister when she's this way.
"Computer, what is struggle?"
COMPUTER: S-T-R-U-G-G-L-E: to proceed with difficulty or with great effort.
"Effort?"
COMPUTER: E-F-F-O-R-T: a positive replacement: a serious attempt to TRY.
"Mama always says to me, 'Don't you try me, boy,"

Sister come'd home lumpy and huddled in her own arms, near quiet ceptin for grunts, moans and swallows chewed behind her lips and the *cries*, give'd off her coat, come'd through the smell of tears on the fur. It might be thought that the *smelling of tears* gives off no cries, but you'd have to know Sister more———cause she doesn't make so many sounds, yet, in everything she do, her voice is locked in it———even the tears on her fur coat. Gramma Shu tell me that I should remember all the things she say to me cause "*they're dying out mongst us.*" And as best, I try. I'm good at remembering voices. Sister don't say much, and I ain't come'd onto her voice that much, but Gramma Shu's voice I got down near enough to fool folks on the telephone. You want to hear it, computer? Computer?

COMPUTER: Please wait! (*no response*)

I went and stood in my doorway.

"Fur coat smelling of tears!"
Gramma Shu mumbled that passing me...
"Pardon me?"
(I weren't thinking.) She shout,
"HER FUR COAT SMELLING OF TEARS!"
...on her way to the bathroom from Sister's room.
I tipped in on Sister whilst her back were to her door and me. She stood by her dresser, wrist-wiping her nose, eyes and lips——— her fur coat lying across her bed, curled up. She held a paper in her hand staring at it———soundlessly mouthing the words from it till she lifted then, in weepings, on re-reading them:

"Dear Baby,
    Have you got two hearts or one?
    If you only got one heart, is that
    heart big enough for two pair of
    size-13 feet? I think not.
                    Bye, Baby."

Sister were know'd to have many boyfriends——but this one... Gramma Shu were coming back, so I hid in a tiny place neath Sister's bed, chin-in-my-knees. Sister crumpled the paper and dropped it——missing the waste basket——onto the floor and kicked the paper under the bed. Gramma Shu come'd—— entered the room. I got dizzy——scared. I scrunched up my face, forced blinking my eyelids cause Gramma Shu stood afore me in a blue haze——she were, somedays, "A *Three-Legged Praying Mantis*," come'd after us. Sister called her, *Mama Knots*. *Mama Knots*, she were: with speckled, knotty hands, palmed over, and she walked on a knotted old cane that *lived!*——wiggled out from her knotted hand like a long, extended knotted finger. She pointed, urged, spelled out and disciplined us with it, marked time and put memorable periods after her words with that knot.

"Oh, Gramma Shu..."
Sister say:
"I don't want to see nothing ever again, no more. He's leaving me."

Gramma Shu don't want to hear it, say:
"*You ain't saying nothing, girl...saying the wrong thing. Hush!*"

Gramma Shu were trying to wipe Sister's face when Sister snatched herself away to go stand and look into the sun, but her eyes so full of tears——

"*You ain't blinding even your own heart, girl! Get your eyes out of the sun!*"

Gramma Shu shouted at whatever Sister trying, "*Ain't gonna work.*" Then Sister run from the sun, say she "leaving," and Gramma Shu grab up Sister's fur coat, following her, quick-tipping on the *echo* give off from the *smelling of tears*. I come out from under the bed and run to my room——hid again. I wanted to cry, but I didn't want nobody to hear me. I talked to myself

——everything felt crazy. I were crazy. Gramma Shu's blue-haze
voice fussed within my thoughts:

"Crazy! No, you ain't crazy, Kitten Face. I been talking to
myself...mymymy...
There is a THRONE!
In this world
What we might
Circle around
Clap your hands on it!
"That's why we talking to ourselves. **A Throne!** child. You
might burst out anytime the Throne be on your mind, singing or
crying to yourself, forgetting that people are around——like when
you got something in you whilst you walking in the streets singing
inside your mouth and you get to a high point in your feelings and you
blurt it "**OUT!**" Well now. How people know you ain't crazy when
they hear that from you? They don't——and they do."

I moaned. Gramma Shu stepped my thoughts:

"I moan——lots...
Moaning is the mule to heaven
Long laboured and pure from hollerin'.
The women that come'd for tea could catch their breath on my
moaning——would rest you up."

She moaned for Grandpa Chas:

"Cold were the tears stuck your Grandpa Charley's hair neath
my chin. Muh. Charley twists all the covers about him, wrapped himself into a husk. Called out, in all manner of fever, called out
names——some ancient——some knowed: a brother, an uncle, old
aunt, his papa's and the neighbour girl's name...."

She wandered on this...lost me in her thoughts, lost me in a
blue haze, and in the haze:

An old man got on a bus and sit down across from Gramma
Shu and me——on the long front seat——sit down burying a

stare in the floor, and singing a very low, deep "O"...holding it an ever! Little old ladies moved away from the area, waving their hands from their wrists like they were scooting flies. Gramma Shu told me not to look at the man. He wouldn't look up, so I thought he were crazy——then he smiled at the floor, the smile jumped off onto it, and the man followed his smile right up into my face.

I giggled——cause Gramma Shu know'd I would——giggled 'Out!' over my thoughts, over her fussing voice within me—— blue.

I wanted my sister's note, and when the coast were clear, I sneaked back under her bed and got the bunched-up paper... sneaked with it out of the room and come'd running to Mama's computer, cause I can't read and talks back when you talk.

"Oh, computer..."

I tried to press the paper flat as I could, but my self were as wrinkled as the paper.

"I...tried to press out the wrinkles for you, computer. If I press the paper up against your face, will you read it for me? Computer? Computer?"

COMPUTER: I cannot read. (*repeat*) I cannot read.

Scream-touched, trouble took up with Gramma Shu whilst she and I were seated peeling potatoes——discouragement come'd on her lips. To get *trouble* to pass, she called on *little ancientnesses* in herself. She come'd steadfast, have sayings on it: *House cleaning for the spirit*...she mumbled it to herself and to whatever she acknowledged to be about her——empty chairs, opened cupboard doors and talked to the shelves——the potatoes. A pink baby rattler with a baby-blue handle lie afore her on the kitchen table what she grabbed——rattling and stood up shouting: 'Happyhappyhappy!'——pat her breasts, her breath sucked up *hesitations*, and sang in fits around the table, she done. She shout:

"*Sing all the voices what oppose in your bosom. Mighty movement'll come. Sing out your fears and night-slurred yelps for even not the Gramma Shu you and your sister ignore someday'll no longer be here for you to hide behind.*"

Her arms flailing a remembered gesture...smeared it on her apron and she strut a long neck what held up a *countenance of reflective beam.* Her eyes have an agreement in them——grabbed at a sudden movement. She swallowed the *beam*...and, seeing nothing further of the movement, continued peeling potatoes, with grey glances towards the corner every now and then where she seen it——till a meanness straightened her into a squinting stare. She say:

"*Charley Tate, is that you?*"

She let her stare drift about the kitchen, left it in the air when her head dropped. Finished the potatoes. She dumped ground beef into a bowl on the table, then, breaking an egg on the bowl's lip, added it.

"*You picked me out for your girl, Charley.*"

She punched the ground-meat-and-egg mixture, squeezed it tween her fingers:

"*Why you do that, Charley?*"

She determined, without measure or count: dusted the meat with Parmesan cheese, dry mustard, bread crumbs, salt, ginger and marjoram——black ground pepper.

"*I were a silly girl, Charley...Loved music——grow'd up with katydids, fireflies, night mists and loons' songs in my ears——but never a man's till yours. I went with your song.*"

She peeled an apple onto the mixture, tinincy cut garlic, onion, crushed pineapple and added a fistful of raisins. This she squeezed tween her fingers again, made a mound in the bowl, then punched a bit off and rolled the meat into round shapes. Says:

"*A man's song might pluck any girl, but a girl ain't supposed to be plucked by any man's song.*"

She placed the meatballs in a dish and spread chutney over it:

"*She fourteen years old, that girl…. Sister just fourteen, and any man sung for her——it ain't right, Charley. I've lived long enough to see everything I been taught, every right I learnt, disappear through the generations!*"

Gramma Shu turned to me:

"Son?"

She swelled on it: "*Your Grandpa Charley Tate…mymymy…*" Her talk sprang after itself:

"*Contagious man——played trumpet, brought us an echo of The Promise!——Contagious man!*"

Her voice freed itself from her in hicupped laughter similar as fallen leaves do whilst you sweeping them——*they skips the broom:*

"*Charley…Mmmmm!*"

She put the meat dish in the oven…and when it was cooked, Gramma Shu set the table with the food and shook the rattler around it——the family sat——she walked around the table shaking the rattler and humming whilst we ate, stopping back of Sister occasionally and rolling her head in figure eights.

Sister carried a secret thing. At first I thought she stole some of Mama's food the way she'd rub at her stomach…but Mama never say a thing. Nothing about missing food. Mama counts everything——it weren't food. Besides, Sister talked to her stomach. It were a fascinating secret cause it were everywhere about her…has a walk to it: stiff-shift and wobble——had a smell to it too, and she'd sneak off to a quiet place with it——a quiet place inside herself. Across the table from me, she were gone to it. Her eyes give nothing back to you...whatever come'd by them, her eyes give nothing back. Even not when I waved in her face———nothing.

I imagined her without eyes: I imagined tiny purple martins flying in and out of her eye sockets, and chirping echoes come'd from the inside holes———all kind of echoes. I imagined the birds flying with worms in their beaks and perching on the ledges of her eye sockets...leaving the worms inside them, then flying away so fast they leave loose feathers floating about Sister's nose———it tickled me. She sneezed but didn't even blink——— she so private. Mama talked down through the holes, say:

"You eating like a bird again, girl. I'm gonna have to give you a physic you keep this up. You can leave the table now."

Sister got up from the table as if summoned from some place, yet been told to leave. I slid from my seat...followed her to the kitchen doorway and watched her stiff-shift wobbling her secret away to her room. Mama reminded me:

"Robert Alex, Jr.? You weren't excused from nowhere, boy." I turned to Mama, and as I sat back down, asked her if I could HAVE WHAT SISTER LEFT ON HER PLATE? Papa put a firm squeeze on my shoulder whenever I tried to ask for something too loud.

Everyone kept bowed as we ate. I were jittery in my chair cause in my plate I saw Papa in my room punishing me. His chewing come'd his footsteps, his hollering at me. I fought gainst his "YOUUUuuuuuu!" Closed my eyes on him, I closed off my hearing to all but Gramma Shu's rattling about the table. I tried to "Ponder pleasant platitudes and attributes," by centring her voice in my thinking: her rattling were an antenna tween me and my memories of stories she made up: "Muffin and the Blueberry"——— "Andrea and the Bird Song." I liked that one. Gramma Shu made that up out of a bird on the wallpaper in my room, what her voice took up with and told whilst I stared at it.

"Now you listen, Kitten Face, and don't you go to sleep afore I finish. You might be a reciter one day and I want you to understand how you're to do it. First, you anchor yourself in some great symbol and pour forth."

She told the story once and requested,

"Now you liked that, didn't you? We storytellers in this family. You see how to do it?"

I scooted back to my chair, squinted up that I were *born of an oak tree and tween tree roots!* I relaxed/were there, and told her the story back:

In the morning of my life there were a very strong want. I would come to this place of my birth and sing of all the things I thought were very nice and special. All the birds would sing with me and I thought that I were the one who controlled the birds. But of course I couldn't control the the fact that the birds would all go away in the wintertime.

Some of the birds didn't go and I were always trying to get them to sing with me but in the winter that is very hard to do, especially if the birds are cold and unhappy because of the weather. I tried very hard to make the birds happy. I danced——which I couldn't do too well cause my legs were too fat. And my jaws wiggled and shook me onto blurs when I danced a stomp or hopped.

The birds would twitter and giggle over the branches at me but never sing. I would throw rocks at the branches *to wake them up!* But that didn't work. I blew my police whistle at them——threw streamers at them, and I stuck out my Halloween tongues at them. But no use! Then the winter were over and the other birds returned. WELL! The birds began to sing again. *"GLORIOUSLY SING!"* I sang as well with them. I composed a spring gesture: went bird-wild, flinging my wings to my music, and the birds all joined in...I were in control once again.

But it didn't work. A ghost breath in me broke up my squinting...

In the centre of my plate, *Papa were standing in the doorway to my room, surrounded by fire and smoke*, and wiping his eyes on fist-knuckles. I could handle it———put my eyes on the case.

I say through spit-sprinkles, through Papa's pointing at me, grunting and wired pupils:

"Papa! I were having a scary dream!"

———And he softened,

"It's all right...What were your dream about? Tell your papa."

"It were a giant computer, Papa...wanted to talk to me and I were scared as when you tell me 'NO!'"

"Now I don't say 'No' to you that much. You a good, boy———most of the time. And don't shout. Your sister's trying to sleep. What the computer say, Son?"

"It ask me what I want to be. And I say, I won't tell it."

Papa come'd to acting all the time, act like he the computer, say:

"T-R-U-S-T me."

"I ain't telling you. I can't tell you."

"Why?"

"Cause you gonna laugh at me."

"No I will not...Try me. Trust me. Respond please. Please respond."

"I got to be dead to be what I want to be."

"Meaning...What do you mean?"

"You won't laugh?"

"Can I laugh?"

"Oh, Computer, I ain't never heard you laugh. To laugh is...laughing...Computer?...Papa, stop teasing!"

"T-R-U-S-T me... Please respond...What do you want to be when you grow up?"

"I want to be a Jedi pilot——and there ain't no one alive like them until the future."

"Growing up is the future."

"Jedi's is farther up-beyond of the future."

"Farther up-beyond of?"

"Yes. So I got to die, and wait until their time to live comes around."

"Where will you go to wait?"

"I'll go be with Grandpa Tate...He said I could...could come and live with him wherever, with him always...live with him even not in the 'WHERES.'"

"Farther up-beyond OF?"

My fork fell off my plate onto the floor. I never heard it. Papa's fist come'd crashing down on the table:

"BOY, WHAT YOU DREAMING IN THE FOOD FOR!?"

Purple martins perched on and pecked at Sister's plate—— took it off with them when I slide down off my chair to pick up my fork. Gramma Shu rattled out of the room after that...left Papa staring at Mama's bowed head——staring at her and chewing like he were eating cold Crisco.

——Gramma Shu, rattling echoes.

I were sent directly to my room after dinner. Papa were to come up and *see me*. I went to thinking about Sister. I reasoned that the thing secret, she had, she wore neath her dress. She were lately placing hands on it and giggling to herself. When her secret weren't neath her dress, it were in her gazing, were cuddled in her arms, were in her hair as she ran her hands through it holding it up to the 'WHERES' for viewing——she smelled of it. Mama told her:

"You smell of something secret, Sister. You'd better be careful."

And when Gramma Shu noticed,

"Sister been removing herself!"

...I tried to talk with Sister...asked her questions:

"What's your secret...won't you tell me, please——huh?"

I'd climb her knees and fuss hug-over her stomach, put my ear in Sister's mouth,

"Will you...?"

...hear her sucking stuff off her gums, and I'd ask her again:

"——Huh...what's your secret?"

I made fists and stuck them in her jaws like earphones. I stuck my eyes just short afore her lips...watched a fish looking pout take shape in them. Sister say,

"Were his words, Robert Alex."

She say it *echosome*, like she ain't have a face to put with him.

Echoed Gramma Shu,

"Heart-searchings! Feelings in the dark's what you got left. You ain't in no struggle, girl. She never seen him——feeling around in the dark'll get you heart-searchings!"

Sister tried to hold her off,

"Were his words! He moistened my mouth so I could soft-say——suck in my breath on it——Yes. I were in his hands. It were big on my heart."

Gramma Shu ask me to testify,

"You hear any struggle in that, Robert Alex?"

Sister let loose her *struggle* in my eyes, say, with no blinking in it, say,

"I giggled when I heard his words, and hiccupped on the echo of Mama's warning."

"What words, Sister?"

Then Sister tried me,

"Robert Alex," she say, "When the moons rise in my fingernails to their tips, I'll give you an answer."

Gramma Shu grunted,

"*Mmmm! Not whilst I'm around, huh?*"

Sister lift me down off her knees———moons rising in my fingernails———walk off from me...slow-rocking stiff-shift wobbling most like she were gonna fall foward and squish.

For weeks I went around watching my fingernails. Gramma Shu say, my fingernails come with moon crescents———*rising*. Computer, what is a crescent?

COMPUTER: Please wait. C-R-E-S-C-E-N-T: 1. a shape resembling a segment of a ring tapering to points at the end. 2. something, as a roll or cookie, having this shape. 3. the figure of the moon in its first or last quarter, resembling a segment of a ring tapering to points at the end...

They're right at the bottoms of my fingernails. Gramma Shu says:

"*Little crescents, moons rising.*"

She sometimes holds my whole face in her hands, says,

"*You got such beautiful eyes, Kitten Face. They are great planets, Honey, surrounded by moons, and big enough to keep you out of trouble, boy.*"

I wondered.

Papa seen my eyes as two raisins in a muffin———called me Muffin after the neighbour Lea's twins, Muffin and The Blueberry. I remember:

When I were little, my Papa come'd to tuck me in one night...pushed me over in my bed, he done, so he could sit next of me. For the longest while he sit, look at me and look away...look at me and look away/look at me...like he hiding-'hind his look-away...and I'd giggle into his "Shush, your sister, stop it." And he'd close his eyes, meaning for me to be silent——have a face, bright as the sun you'd see it. I called him: Chief Smile Sit With No Eyes Silent. He shift-scrunch-up close to me and the covers pinched at me. My "OUCH!" scooted him off a bit, pulling the covers loose from my back, what he straightened, asking: "Would you like to say a prayer tonight, Muffin?" My Papa's eyes shined, "Say it, won't you," they asks of me. And I crawled out of bed, got on my knees, next of his sitting, I placed my elbows on his knees and put my hands together. He dipped his head and I stared up into his eyes, what Papa closed, and I closed mine——went into closed-eyes squinting:

"I forgot!"
"Forgot what, Muffin?"
"I forgot His Name!"
"Whose name?"
"I forgot it!"
Papa's hands folded around mine,
"Whose?"
I closed my eyes so tight, trying to remember, it hurt around my nose. A trembling roared in my ears and I burst:
"O! I remember it!"
"Whose?"
Papa say it like, "That's it, go on," and I shout it:
"GOD'S!...I remember It! I remember His Name. I remember."

Papa hugged me up hard to himself, but I pushed-slipped through his arms back to my knees, elbows on his knee and hands clasped together, remembering:

> O God,
> I pinched up a flower
> Neath my nose today
> And smelt You.

Papa's jerk, "UMH!" jerked me, and I fast-climbed his knee. He hugged me harder...put me back to bed and tucked me in. He had tears in his eyes. Maybe Papa will remember this when he comes/Oh-oh...

"YOUUUuuuuuu..."

Dany Laferrière

Why Must a Negro Writer Always Be Political?

First of all, is it essential for a writer to be identified by colour? I have to deal with this kind of question all the time. In the subway, in a restaurant (the bastard eats!), during a match at the stadium, in a taxi.

The cab driver presents himself as Nigerian. That's how he begins the conversation. Of course he hasn't visited his homeland in twenty years. To be more specific, he's African. He wants to make that perfectly clear. If Africa is now made up of disparate pieces, it's because of the colonialists. They're the ones who divided up the land. Needless to say, he's against this division. If he introduces himself as Nigerian, it's because people are always asking him where he comes from exactly. At first he held his ground. He explained that Africa was made up of a single people. The expression *Black Africa* was not only redundant, he would insist; it was politically stupid, a dirty trick, something the Western mind concocted to confuse Africans. In Africa, colour does not exist. When everyone has the same colour, colour disappears. Differences cease. And South Africa? He'd rather not discuss South Africa. This topic makes his blood boil. Each time the subject comes up, he flies into a white rage (*colère noire*). This play on words makes him chuckle. He recalls a client who spoke out in favour of apartheid. He turned without warning, gave the fellow a swift blow in the mouth. The jerk complained, which resulted in a month's lay-off. But he's glad he did it. The judge told him that, in America, we live in a democracy. Everyone has a right to his opinion. He told the judge it wasn't an opinion, the creep's just a bloody racist bastard. He began to scream blue murder. He was tossed out of court. He got a month off, a severe warning. The next time he would lose his licence. If he hadn't created such a ruckus, his lawyer told him, he would have gotten off with a week. He can live with it. He has no regrets. He's got to be careful, though, not to engage in any sensitive conversations with his clients (I rather doubt he tries very hard. I don't say a word). However, if some jerk comes into his cab and makes racist remarks, he can't be expected to keep quiet. He can't let things like that pass. Anyway, if you lose your job you can always find another one. But if you lose your dignity, you've lost everything. It's not because you're forced to work like a slave that you become less human. I am a Negro. I'm proud to be one. He spoke without practically ever turning his head. I'm under the impression he tells this story all the time. It doesn't matter who his passenger is. He eventually turns in my direction. He looks me over. He seems surprised when he sees me.

—I read your book.

He spoke dryly. Expect the worst when a cab driver turns to you and wants to discuss your book. More than likely, he's read it while at the wheel. If this is the case, books with short chapters, lots of dialogue, are advisable. The kind of book I also like to read.

—I'd like to ask you a question.

— Go ahead.

— Why did you write the book?

The question shot out, a projectile dangerously aimed at my forehead. I wasn't expecting it. Normally, when a book's out, it's out. You either like it or you don't. I remain calm. He pretends to look straight ahead. His ears are outrageously cocked. He is obviously listening.

— You don't want to answer. I know how you feel.

He knows bugger-all! Every single Negro in this bloody town thinks each one of his questions strikes like a bomb and will wreak destruction on all of America.

— I wrote the book I was in the mood to write.

His look implies, That was a cute answer; now say what's really on your mind. Instead I ask him a question.

— What's wrong with my book?

My question throws him off. I notice a slight quiver in his neck. He turns towards me. The cab nearly climbs onto the sidewalk.

— It's a traitor's book.

He rams his palms against the steering wheel. He pumps the accelerator pedal. The panel clock shows 2:49 a.m. He remains silent for a while.

— Sometimes I think I know why you wrote that shit. For the money. It's tough out there. I know. Real tough. You get nothing for free, unless you're willing to sell your soul. There'll always be a buyer for that.

— In my case, no need for a buyer...I did it willingly.

— That's it. You've learned the ropes. So no one can tell you what to do.

— There's another way of looking at it.

He looks at me threateningly. He's not the kind of guy you like to contradict. That's quite clear.

— What do you mean?

— All writers are traitors, on some level.

— That's bullshit.

— I mean it's tough for everybody (I hate to use those words). Competition is fierce. When you can't woo them with your know-how, a good striptease will sometimes do the trick.

— Does that mean you have to sell your race?

— Yes.

He eyes me while stepping on the accelerator. He wants to scare me. Where are the cops when you need them?

— I write to gain power. Just like what you're doing right now. You're driving like a madman to scare the shit out of me. It's the same for me. It's a matter of who gets leverage. I'll do anything to gain the advantage.

He's a bit puzzled. I've used his own words against him. He's a violent man. Violence is the only language he understands. He changes his tune a little. I notice something softer in him, almost invisible to the naked eye.

— Why not work in tandem with the reader?

— I don't consider the reader a friend. It's all an illusion. The reader would ask for nothing better than to tell his life story. He's got a story to tell, one he'd like to shout from every rooftop. So, if you want to glue him to a seat for hours while you tell your tale, you'd better come up with a good line. Nothing fancy. It doesn't even have to be very good.

— That's where I disagree.

— I'm listening.

I was in fact listening.

— Why not use all that energy for the benefit of your race?

— That goes against everything that literature stands for.

Talk about hyperbole!

— How's that?

— You don't write to do someone a favour. You must have something to say, you have to want to say it, you have to find ways to say it. In other words, style.

— You mean you don't feel like defending your people, humiliated for centuries!

— Of course I do. It's obvious. But you have to use the right tool. And it won't be literature. At least it won't be good literature.

— Africa has a rich history. Negro writers have a responsibility. They have to convey this knowledge.

— Exactly. I'm a writer in the present tense. I search for traces of the past in the present. Maybe you're right. There are surely Negroes out there quite suited to the task. Let them talk of the beauty that's part of our race. Not me. I don't have the qualifications. I'm only interested in man's fall, his decrepitude, his frustration, the bitterness that keeps men alive.

— Why don't you just admit you're out to make a buck?

— Like everyone else. For me, writing is just something I do to earn a living. Like everyone else. Why aren't engineers, doctors, lawyers ever asked to justify their choice? I'm telling you: I write because I want to make a name for myself, with all the benefits that go along with it. I also write to get laid by luscious young girls. Before, they wouldn't even give me the time of day.

Now he's on the same wavelength. A vein puffs up in his neck. His blood is obviously pumped up.

— But why not meld the two...I mean, make money and pay homage—I know you hate this word—to your people.

— These are irreconcilable opposites. Commercial sense versus good intentions.

— Some people do it.

— You mean Soyinka and his Nobel prize?

— Yes.

— I don't have his talent. That guy'll wind up in all the school books. I'd rather be read by those who despise me. If you beat a horse, I'm not convinced he'll like you; but anytime you're within striking distance, he'll be aware of your presence. Do you know what I mean?

— Yes, but why do you continually fall back on clichés about Negroes?

— It's an open mine. Everyone has a right to work the soil.

— You exploit...

— Just like anybody else. Don't you think all writers do the same thing? A writer is usually a cannibal. He eats people up, digests them, spews them out in words. White, black, yellow or red.

— What a cynical view of things!

— Not really. An ordinary view of things.

— Does that mean you would have preferred being a white writer?

— Not at all, and this has nothing to do with politics. Practically speaking, it's quite interesting being a Negro right now. People are ready to listen to us. It's a new voice. People have had it up to here with the love triangle (you know: the husband, the wife, the lover). They're so hungry for new stories, they'll beg for them. Even the old machine "adultery" needs oiling. Look at the job Spike Lee did in *Jungle Fever*. The same love triangle, except in different colours. The married couple is black, the mistress white. Any change is welcome. We beg you: change something.

— Yeah, but there's a difference. Spike Lee makes films for blacks. You give the impression you're writing for the whites.

— I write for readers rich enough to have the luxury to read. It's easy to forget: reading is a luxury. Three-quarters of humanity has no clue this pastime exists. When Spike Lee says he's making films for blacks, that's bullshit. How can we know in advance who will be interested in our books, our films? There's no way of knowing. It's likely Spike Lee's film touched more whites than blacks.

— Why do you talk about him so much? Jealous?

— I envy his success, not his talent.

— Why, then?

— I've told you. He interests me. His energy. We're different, though; we don't share the same enemy. For him, it's the white race. For me, it's all of America.

— Paranoid?

— Not enough.

He laughs for the first time. Rich laughter, tight at first, than reaching a strident pitch before following a joyful descent, grave, vibrant. Laughter from the pit of the stomach.

— It's quite simple. Why should I love you? You don't love me. It's not because you're black that I should love you. You, the blacks, are the first to scream for my hide.

He turns. He has a serious look, as if he's just understood something.

— I understand. You're going through a bad patch. You'll see. It'll come back.

— What'll come back?

— Well...(he looks a bit embarrassed)...humanist feelings... fraternal...we blacks don't know how to truly hate.... We're deficient in hate chromosomes....

That's the best he can do. The cab stops on the side of the road. I pay, get off. Someone else gets in. The cab jerks forward, speeds away. I watch. The driver starts up a conversation.

— I'm African. More specifically, I'm from Nigeria. If you want my opinion, all blacks are African, we all come from the first Negro, from the first Negress.

Bullshit.

About the Authors

AUSTIN CLARKE was born in Barbados and came to Toronto in 1955, where he attended Trinity College, University of Toronto. He has had a varied and busy career as visiting professor at many American universities, as the organizer of a broadcasting system in Barbados, as managing editor of *Contrast* and as a member of the Ontario Board of  Censors. He has won many literary awards: the Casa de las Americas Literary Prize (1980), the President's Gold Medal from the University of Western Ontario (1965) and the *Saturday Night* Short Story Award (1965).

GEORGE ELLIOTT CLARKE was born in Nova Scotia, a seventh-generation Canadian. He is a graduate of both the University of Waterloo and Dalhousie University. Currently, Clarke is a doctoral candidate in English at Queen's University. He has worked as an editor, researcher, journalist and parliamentary aide. Clarke is the author of three books of poetry,  *Saltucher Spirituals*, *Deeper Blues* and *Whylah Falls*, and the editor of *Fire on the Water*, an anthology of Black Nova Scotian writing.

AFUA COOPER was born in Jamaica and immigrated to Canada in 1980. She obtained her B.A. at the University of Toronto, and is now working on a Ph.D. in history. She has a long and eclectic background in the performing and literary arts. Cooper is the

© 1992 by J.L. Hodgins

author of two books of poetry, *Breaking Chains* and *Red Caterpillar on College Street* (children's poetry), and has given many readings in Canada and the United States. Her poetry is also recorded on various collections including *Woman Talk* and *Poetry Is Not a Luxury*. Cooper has just completed a new book of poems called *Memories Have Tongue*.

CYRIL DABYDEEN ended his formal education at Queen's University with postgraduate degrees in English and in public administration. He has taught for many years at Algonquin College,

and now teaches creative writing (fiction) at the University of Ottawa. He is also a race-relations practitioner, and his work has appeared in numerous periodicals and anthologies in Canada, the U.K., Europe, the Caribbean, India, Malaysia and New Zealand. He was named the Poet Laureate of Ottawa from 1984 to 1987. His books include six collections of poetry and two of short stories. He also edited *A Shapely Fire: Changing the Literary Landscape* (Mosaic Press, 1986). Two novels published with Peepal Tree Press (U.K.) appeared in 1989. His latest work is *Coastland: New and Selected Poems* (Mosaic Press, 1989).

NIGEL DARBASIE was born on the Caribbean island of Trinidad, where he attended Queen's Royal College. In 1969 he moved to Canada, completing his post-secondary education with a B.Sc. degree from the University of Alberta. He has settled on the prairies and is an Edmonton-based writer. His book of poetry, *Last Crossing*, was a finalist in the Writers Guild of Alberta Awards for Excellence. His work has been broadcast on radio, including

the University of Alberta's CJSR, CKUA's "Arts Alberta" and CBC's "Alberta's Anthology." In addition, he has been featured on the Shaw cable television network and on the CBC-TV series, "Dream Seekers." Darbasie has performed at arts festivals and at cultural and literary events. He has been published in various anthologies, most recently *A Land of Many Voices*, and has been featured in a book and video series on Alberta writers.

CECIL FOSTER was born in Barbados and immigrated to Canada in 1979. He has worked as a reporter for the *Toronto Star*, as business reporter for the *Globe and Mail*, and was the editor of *Contrast*. Well known as one of Canada's top business reporters, Foster is now a senior editor at the *Financial Post*. He is the author of *No Man in the House*.

NORMA DE HAARTE was born in Guyana, where she worked as a schoolteacher until she immigrated to Canada. After obtaining her B.A., she returned to Guyana and worked as a guidance officer with the Ministry of Education. During this time, she had the opportunity to explore and become intimately familiar with the interior of Guyana. In 1982, she returned to Canada, where she writes and teaches. She is the author of *Guyana Betrayal*.

CLAIRE HARRIS was born in Trinidad and came to Canada in 1966. She settled in Calgary, where she teaches English in the separate school system. In 1975, during a visit to Nigeria, she began to write for publication. She was the poetry editor of the Alberta quarterly *Dandelion*, from 1981 to '89, and she has been a member of the Writers Guild of Alberta since its inception. Her first book, *Fables from Women's Quarters* (Williams/Wallace), won a Commonwealth Award in 1985. Her third book, *Travelling to Find a Remedy*, won the Writers Guild of Alberta Award for poetry and the first Alberta Culture Poetry Prize in 1986. In 1980, *The Conception of Winter* won an Alberta special award for poetry. Her forthcoming books are *Under Black Light* and *Birth of an Angel*.

LAWRENCE HILL is an author from Oakville. He has worked for the *Globe and Mail* and the *Winnipeg Free Press*. His short fiction has appeared in *Exile, Descant* and *Blood and Aphorisms*. His first novel, *Greatness My Son*, is to be published by Turnstone Press in the fall of 1992. Hill is currently working on more short stories and a second novel.

DANY LAFERRIÈRE was born in Port-au-Prince, Haiti, where he practiced journalism under the dictatorial reign of Duvalier. When a friend, also a journalist, was found murdered in 1976, Laferrière took the hint and went into exile in Canada in 1978, where he wrote his first novel, *Comment faire l'amour avec un nègre sans se fatiguer* (How to Make Love to a Negro Without Getting Tired), which has been translated into several languages. The film version of

the book was released in forty-five countries. He is also the author of *Eroshima* and *L'odeur du café*. He lives in Miami and Montreal.

MOLARA OGUNDIPE-LESLIE is a Nigerian-born writer, poet, scholar and literary critic. She is a founding member of the International Women for a Meaningful Summit and co-founder of the Association of African Research and Development and  Women in Nigeria. She has been a major figure in academia since the 1960s, a leading scholar in women's studies and women-in-development. Ogundipe-Leslie's biography and poems have appeared in several authoritative anthologies, including *The Penguin Book of Modern African Poetry*, *Voices from 20th-Century Africa*, the *Heinemann International Book of African Poetry* and *African Women Poets*, edited by Frank Chapasula. Her collection *Sew the Old Days and Other Poems* was published in 1985, and her work has appeared in various magazines and anthologies.

Ogundipe-Leslie has innovated a new-yet-old type of poetry that harks back to the traditional performance modes of her Yoruba culture: the call and refrain, the play with sound at its many levels as the mind rises naturally from speech to incantation to song (a style surviving in the black sermon); and the active participation of her audience in the creative process. She sometimes calls this form "living poetry," not only because it is a vibrant tradition in Africa, but because it is also a form that draws on the immediate vitality of her audience.

ROZENA MAART was born in District Six, Cape Town, South Africa, and has lived in England, Colombia and, since 1989, in Canada. A writer, poet, public speaker and sessional lecturer in Canada and the United States, she publishes regularly in journals and magazines. In 1991, she published *Talk About It!*, a poetry and essay collection. She is currently teach-

ing at the University of Ottawa. Her areas of interest are black consciousness, psychoanalysis and feminist theory.

Born in Jamaica, **MAKEDA SILVERA** spent her early years in Kingston before immigrating to Canada. Writing has always been a major interest. She began in journalism, working with Toronto's *Contrast* and *Share*, and was a former editorial collective member of *Fireweed*, a feminist quarterly. Her stories, articles and essays have appeared in numerous journals. She is the author of two books, *Silenced,* a collection of interviews with Caribbean domes-

tic workers in Canada, and *Remembering G,* her first book of fiction. She also edited *Piece of My Heart*, writings by lesbians of colour living in North America. Silvera is co-founder of Sister Vision Press, the first press for women of colour in Canada, where she works as managing editor.

FREDERICK WARD is an author, playwright, composer and actor. He studied music in Los Angeles and has taught at Dalhousie University. His published works include *Riverslip*, *Nobody Called*  *Me Mine*, *A Room Full of Balloons* and *The Curing Berry*, a collection of prose poetry. Ward's compositions, poetry, plays and theatrical performances have won him international recognition. In May 1992, Dalhousie University will award him an honorary LL.D. Born in Kansas City, Missouri, he now lives in Blockhouse, Nova Scotia, and Montreal.

Lois Segal

About the Editor

AYANNA BLACK was born in Jamaica and lived in England before immigrating to Canada in 1964. Her work has been anthologized in various books, such as *SP/ELLes* and *Women & Words*. She is one of the founding members of *Tiger Lily*, Canada's first magazine by women of colour, and president of Canadian Artists' Network—Black Artists in Action (CAN-BAIA). She often  contributes to *Fuse* magazine, writing on cultural issues. She is the author of *No Contingencies* and co-author of *Linked Alive*. Black has given many poetry readings in Canada and the United States, and in 1991 six European cities for *Linked Alive*. Currently, she is working on a new poetry collection called *Invoking the Spirits*.

© 1992 by J.L. Hodgins